Children, Teachers and Learning Series

General Editor: Cedric Cullingford

Children's Mathematical Thinking in the Primary Years

Titles in the Children, Teachers and Learning series:

Children's Mathematical Thinking in the Primary Years

Perspectives on Children's Learning

Edited by Julia Anghileri

continuum
LONDON • NEW YORK

Continuum

The Tower Building
11 York Road
London SE1 7NX

15 East 26th Street
New York
NY 10010

www.continuumbooks.com

First published 1995

Reprinted 1999, 2003, 2005

British Library Cataloguing in Publication Data
A catalogue record for this book is available from the British Library.

ISBN 0-304-33258-5 (hardback)
     0-304-33260-7 (paperback)

Typeset by Create Publishing Services Ltd, Bath, Avon
Printed and bound in Great Britain by
Biddles Ltd, King's Lynn, Norfolk

Contents

List of Contributors

JULIA ANGHILERI is Head of the Mathematics Department at Homerton College, University of Cambridge involved in the initial and in-service training of teachers as well as research in Mathematics Education. She has published a number of articles in professional and research journals relating to children learning mathematics. She has an international reputation for the work she has done on children's understanding of multiplication and associated aspects of mathematical language.

Other authors all contribute to Mathematics Education courses in undergraduate and postgraduate initial training and to in-service programmes for mathematics at Homerton College. The following brief notes identify some of their expertise.

LYNDON BAKER is a freelance advisor for *Mathematics Teaching*, a technical author, and developer of curriculum materials for mathematics teaching. He is an active member of the Association of Teachers of Mathematics and is currently involved in a range of initial and in-service training courses, both school and college based.

LIBBY JARED was Head of Mathematics at a secondary school and is now Senior Lecturer and Homerton College Information Technology (IT) Co-ordinator. Libby has produced IT study packs for initial training students covering all aspects of IT in primary schools and is involved in the induction of students and teachers into the applications of computing in children's learning.

DON MACKAY teaches and co-ordinates mathematics at Parkway Middle School in Suffolk. As well as being a part-time member of the teaching team at Homerton College, he has been invited as a teacher advisor to contribute to working groups involved with the introduction of the Mathematics National Curriculum.

ANNIE OWEN has teaching experience in both primary and secondary schools in the UK and abroad. She is Senior Lecturer in Mathematics Education and College Co-ordinator for mathematics curriculum courses. Annie contributes regularly to the journal *Junior Education* and has written several books for teachers.

LAURIE ROUSHAM was Head Teacher of a primary school involved in the CAN Curriculum Project under the direction of Hilary Shuard. He is Senior Lecturer in Mathematics Education and is currently involved in research based at Kings College in London. As a member of the National Curriculum Council B Committee he contributed to discussion and documentation accompanying the introduction of the England and Wales – National Curriculum Statutory Orders.

TIM ROWLAND is Senior Lecturer in Mathematics and Mathematics Education and is the Director of INSET at Homerton College. As well as being an active and enthusiastic mathematician, he has a well-established reputation in initial and in-service training of primary teachers and is currently engaged in research into children's mathematical thinking. Tim is a regular contributor to journals in Mathematics Education.

ANNE THWAITES is Senior Lecturer in Mathematics and Mathematics Education involved in many aspects of the initial and in-service training of primary teachers. Her expertise with IT applications in the teaching of mathematics ranges from infant and primary school children to mathematics undergraduates and number theory. Anne is Director of Curriculum and Professional Studies for the BEd degree.

DAVID WHITEBREAD is an ex-primary school teacher and is Senior Lecturer in Psychology at Homerton College. His experiences with postgraduate and initial training students as well as his involvement with local infant schools offer a balanced expertise in the theory and practice of education for young children.

Foreword

The books in this series stem from the conviction that all those who are concerned with education should have a deep interest in the nature of children's learning. Teaching and policy decisions ultimately depend on an understanding of individual personalities accumulated through experience, observation and research. Too often in recent years decisions on the management of education have had little to do with the realities of children's lives, and too often the interest shown in the performance of teachers, or in the content of the curriculum, has not been balanced by an interest in how children respond to either. The books in this series are based on the conviction that children are not fundamentally different from adults, and that we understand ourselves better by our insight into the nature of children.

The books are designed to appeal to *all* those who are interested in education and who take it as axiomatic that anyone concerned with human nature, culture or the future of civilization is interested in education – in the individual process of learning, as well as what can be done to help it. While each book draws on recent findings in research and is aware of the latest developments in policy, each is written in a style that is clear, readable and free from the jargon that has undermined much scholarly writing, especially in such a relatively new field of study.

Although the audience to be addressed includes all those concerned with education, the most important section of the audience is made up of professional teachers, the teachers who continue to learn and grow and who need both support and stimulation. Teachers are very busy people, whose energies are taken up in coping with difficult circumstances. They deserve material that is stimulating, useful and free of jargon and is in tune with the practical realities of classrooms.

Each book is based on the principle that the study of education is a discipline in its own right. There was a time when the study of the principles of learning and the individual's response to his or her environment was a collection of parts of other disciplines – history, philosophy, linguistics, sociology and psychology. That time is assumed to be over and the books address those who are interested in the study of children and how they respond to their environment.

Each book is written both to enlighten the readers and to offer practical help to develop their understanding. They therefore not only contain accounts of what we understand about children, but also illuminate these accounts by a series of examples, based on observation of practice. These examples are designed not as a series of rigid steps to be followed, but to show the realities on which the insights are based.

Most people, even educational researchers, agree that research on children's learning has been most disappointing, even when it has not been completely missing. Apart from the general lack of a 'scholarly' educational tradition, the inadequacies of such study come about because of the fear of approaching such a complex area as children's inner lives. Instead of answering curiosity with observation, much educational research has attempted to reduce the problem to simplistic solutions, by isolating a particular hypothesis and trying to improve it, or by trying to focus on what is easy and 'empirical'. These books try to clarify the real complexities of the problem, and are willing to be speculative.

The real disappointment with educational research, however, is that it is very rarely read or used. The people most at home with children are often unaware that helpful insights can be offered to them. The study of children and the understanding that comes from self-knowledge are too important to be left to obscurity. In the broad sense real 'research' is carried out by all those engaged in the task of teaching or bringing up children.

All the books share a conviction that the inner worlds of children repay close attention, and that much subsequent behaviour and attitudes depend upon the early years. They also share the conviction that children's natures are not markedly different from those of adults, even if they are more honest about themselves. The process of learning is reviewed as the individual's close and idiosyncratic involvement in events, rather than the passive reception of, and processing of, information.

Cedric Cullingford

Introduction
JULIA ANGHILERI

This book presents perspectives on children's thinking in school mathematics and explores ways in which learning may be facilitated when teachers are invited to share the depth of analysis provided by research. It is written by teachers who have enjoyed the opportunity to reflect on some aspect of mathematics learning and to develop some expertise in a given area. It is written for teachers, students and interested parents to introduce them to topics of relevance in Mathematics Education today.

The content of this book addresses some of the major issues concerning teachers of children in the primary (elementary) school today that are identified in the curricular requirements of school mathematics. There has been no attempt to provide a comprehensive analysis of all school mathematics but the snapshots that are included reflect the interests and enthusiasms of a group of individuals who work at the same institution, Homerton College, University of Cambridge in the UK. Throughout the book, authors share their observations and analysis of children's mathematical thinking and learning and offer practical examples to support the classroom teacher. Since the chapters are independent of one another, the reader should feel free to 'dip into' the text in any order and refer to those aspects of mathematics teaching that they find most relevant and fascinating.

Children as thinkers

This century has witnessed enormous changes and challenges in mathematics teaching from the chalk and slate arithmetic of our grandfathers to the computer and electronic calculators now found in every classroom. From a time when whole classes were only expected to master standard skills in number and measuring, through 'discovery learning' to the current focus on problem solving, addressing the needs of a fast changing technological society, teachers have been faced with the challenge of adapting their teaching approaches and addressing new curricular requirements and recommendations.

Although these chapters are based on experiences in the United Kingdom, they reflect developments across the developed world. As well as references to *Mathematics in the National Curriculum for England and Wales* (SCAA, 1994) specific references are made to the *USA Curriculum and Evaluation Standards for School Mathematics* (NCTM, 1989) and the *Curriculum and Assessment in Scotland – National Guidelines: Mathematics 5–14* (SOED, 1991). In each of these curricula there is an emphasis on the development of children as mathematical thinkers, confident in their ability to solve problems and communicate effectively in preparation for a role in society today.

> The ... curriculum should emphasise the development of children's mathematical thinking and reasoning abilities. An individual's future uses and needs for mathematics make the ability to think, reason and solve problems a primary goal for the study of mathematics ... the curriculum must take seriously the goal of instilling in students a sense of confidence in their ability to think and communicate mathematically. (NCTM, 1989, p. 18)

Although there are some differences in terminology across the different nations the parallels between nursery and kindergarten, and primary and elementary, are substantial with the mathematical learning of young children involving universal considerations reflected in the content of this book. In mathematics teaching today across the developed world, there is a focus on the way in which children learn as active problem solvers, articulating their thoughts and learning to make logical connections as they acquire the language and skills relevant to society today. Readers will recognize references to their national criteria and the references to age ranges and detailed content that are included. Readers will also be impressed by the consistency of views held on mathematics teaching in the primary school.

The mathematics curriculum

Starting with an overview of the changes that have taken place in mathematics teaching in this twentieth century, the chapters of this book will consider some of the most significant aspects of change, the rationale behind them, and implications for the reflective classroom teacher's practice.

In the first chapter, there is a brief outline of the technological developments that have had a significant impact on the mathematics to be learned in schools, and the way such learning can be achieved. There are acknowledgements of the influences that psychologists have had in changing teaching approaches from 'drill and practice' exercises that dominated mathematics learning earlier this century to children's active participation in problem solving tasks, involvement in discussion and emphasis on communication.

The next chapter considers early experiences young children have in learning mathematics. David Whitebread presents evidence that mathematics learning can be enhanced by considering parallels with language learning in a manner termed **'emergent mathematics'**. He considers the way in which children learn, he identifies difficulties they may experience with school mathematics as contrasted with home mathematics and he draws on the work of developmental psychologists to support an alternative approach, enabling children to learn in a meaningful way:

> The teacher's job is to organise and provide the sorts of experiences which enable pupils to construct and develop their own understanding of mathematics. (DES and Welsh Office, 1989, p. C2)

Continuing with this theme of meaningful mathematics, consideration is next given to enquiry and investigation where children are encouraged to draw mathematical relationships from 'real-life' contexts:

> Teaching through enquiry (learning through posing and attempting to solve problems and tackle investigations) emphasises the role of pupils as active thinkers with some control over the scope and direction of their work. Pupils are encouraged to ask themselves questions, to decide what information they need, how to proceed and how best to report their findings. (SOED, 1991, p. 57)

In his chapter on **investigational activities** with 10- and 11-year-olds, Don Mackay analyses the teachers choice of starting point for investigations and the consequent mathematical procedures with which children become involved. He considers the pupils' ability to discard 'noise' from the information given, and to abstract a mathematical relationship from 'real-life' information, constructing mathematical relationships through representations of differing types.

Representation in mathematics develops beyond pictorial and diagrammatic illustrations as the language and symbols are formalised to provide a concise and powerful means of communication. There are two chapters on **language** that reflect its important role in children's development as mathematical thinkers. Tim Rowland considers the role of 'talk' in children's learning of the **language of mathematics** and uses conversations with and between children to illustrate the way a teacher may reflect on the manner in which thoughts may be expressed and the thinking that is involved in children's developing understanding.

> Discussion (learning by sharing ideas and talking things over) allows pupils to bring partly formed mathematical ideas out into the open where they can be shared and modified and misunderstandings can be resolved. The teacher's role is to provide contexts which motivate discussion and to encourage pupils to express their own perspectives and difficulties with confidence ... comparing methods of calculation, for example, or explaining how an answer was obtained, can strengthen understanding of the processes involved. (SOED, 1991, p. 57)

> Young children learn through verbal communication; it is important, therefore, to provide opportunities for them to 'talk mathematics.' Interacting with classmates helps children construct knowledge, learn other ways to think about ideas, and clarify their own thinking. (NCTM, 1989, p. 26)

He also considers the potential of meta-language to reveal aspects of children's mathematical thinking and the way pronouns are used in a different (and revealing) manner by teachers and by children. This and his discussion on children's use of 'hedges' to convey a sense of uncertainty in their thinking will undoubtedly provoke teachers to listen to themselves and their children more closely in their future interactions in the classroom.

In a further chapter on language, Julia Anghileri looks in detail at the **meanings of symbols** in arithmetic, the conflict and confusion that may arise if meanings are not shared and the teacher's role in enabling children to understand and use the more formal definitions that are the key to mathematics as a powerful and concise means of communication.

(Pupils) should be given the opportunity to talk about their work, and to compare their ideas with others. Pupils should be taught to explain their thinking, ask questions and follow alternative suggestions to support their developing reasoning . . . [In] developing mathematical language . . . pupils should be taught to understand the language of number . . . talk about their work, responding to and asking questions. (SCAA, 1994, p. 3)

Middle school students . . . should have many opportunities to use language to communicate their mathematical ideas. The communication process requires students to reach agreement about the meanings of words and to recognize the crucial importance of commonly shared definitions. (NCTM, 1989, p. 78)

The focus of this chapter is the symbolic representations of the operations of arithmetic: addition, subtraction, multiplication and division, all familiar to every school teacher, perhaps to the extent that informal language is able to persist and act as an inhibitor to progress beyond naive concepts and strategies. By raising teachers awareness of the complexities involved in the language of arithmetic, they may become better able to support pupils learning through discussion and the negotiation of meanings to further enhance pupils understanding.

Instruction should help children connect their intuitions and informal language to operations, including the mathematical language and symbols of each operation. (NCTM, 1989, p. 41)

Young pupils' mathematical abilities are most likely to be developed in situations which they can readily understand and discuss. As they progress, they can build meaningful links between the language of number and their own informal understanding of number. (SOED, 1991, p. 53)

Calculators have been the cause of much controversy since their availability to children became commonplace both in school and at home. There is no question that a calculator can provide an important personal tool to assist in problem solving and Laurie Rousham describes ways in which teachers can gain insight into children's thinking when calculator activities provide the basis for discussion.

Contrary to the fears of many, the availability of calculators and computers has expanded students' capability of performing calculations. There is no evidence to suggest that the availability of calculators makes students dependent on them for simple calculations. Students should be able to decide when they need to calculate and whether they need an exact or approximate answer. Students should have a balanced approach to calculation, be able to choose appropriate procedures and judge the validity of those answers. (NCTM, 1989, p. 8)

Calculators increase calculating power and widen the range of calculations which pupils can manage; they give scope for developing insight into number and its uses in problems and enquiries. (SOED, 1991, p. 6)

As well as calculators being readily available, most children have access to computers both in the classroom and at home. The impact of this technology is evident throughout society and skills in **information handling** present specific targets for mathematics teaching.

Collecting, organising, describing, displaying, and interpreting data, as well as making decisions and predictions on the basis of that information are skills that are increasingly important in a society based on technology and communication. These processes are particularly appropriate for young children because they can be used to solve problems that are inherently interesting, represent significant applications of mathematics to practical questions, and offer rich opportunities for mathematical enquiry. (NCTM, 1989, p. 54)

Libby Jared and Anne Thwaites present practical examples to illustrate the way teachers may help children develop the skills and understanding necessary to appreciate the facility and power provided by computer methods in handling data.

The Scottish National Guidelines: Mathematics 5–14 (1991) list four attainment outcomes for **information handling**:

The pupil recognizes, understands, uses and applies the concepts, facts and techniques across the four strands to:
collect information ... organise information ... display information ... interpret information (p. 21)

The chapter by Lyndon Baker on **problem solving** considers the outcome of activities undertaken by teachers, children and student teachers and addresses the question 'What is mathematical problem solving?' By eliciting the views of teachers who have themselves actively participated in such activities and by identifying issues that arise, the reader will come to reflect on the relevance of a problem solving approach to mathematics teaching in the early years of schooling.

Such importance is placed on problem solving in the USA NCTM Standards (1989) that they quote a noted industrial mathematician, Henry Pollak (1987), in summarizing the mathematical expectations for new employees in industry:

- The ability to set up problems with the appropriate operations
- Knowledge of a variety of techniques to approach and work on problems
- Understanding of the underlying mathematical features of a problem
- The ability to work with others on problems
- The ability to see the applicability of mathematical ideas to common and complex problems
- Preparations for open problem situations, since most real problems are not well-formulated
- Belief in the utility and value of mathematics. (NCTM, 1989, p. 4)

These Standards also lay emphasis on problem solving as a means as well as a goal of instruction and list 'Mathematics as Problem Solving' as an identified standard in all the grades K–12.

> Tackling problems, both of the practical 'real-life' sort, and within mathematics itself, *motivates and requires* the learning of further skills and the development of greater understanding. (DES and Welsh Office, 1989, p. D1)

Scottish National Guidelines: Mathematics 5–14 (1991) identify Problem Solving and Enquiry as one of the attainment outcomes for mathematics teaching for 5–14-year-olds and recommend that 'Mathematics should be viewed in the widest sense as a problem solving activity'. The guidelines go on (p. 12) to note that 'where pupils are involved in problem solving and enquiry, they will be challenged to think about what they are doing, to question and to explain.'

The final chapter addresses the opportunities that exist for developing children's thinking in **algebra**. In this chapter, Annie Owen provides many examples of the way children's understanding may develop in the early years by creating, observing and generalizing patterns:

> It is essential that in grades 5–8 students explore algebraic concepts in an informal way to build a foundation for the subsequent formal study of algebra. Such informal exploration should emphasise physical models,

data, graphs, and other mathematical representations rather than facility with formal algebraic manipulation ... Learning to recognise patterns and regularities in mathematics and make generalisations about them requires practice and experience. ... By integrating informal algebraic experiences throughout the K–8 curriculum, students will develop confidence in using algebra to represent and solve problems. (NCTM, 1989, p. 102)

[The] aspect of mathematics which enables pupils to explore and explain the structure, patterns and relationships within mathematics is an important factor in enabling them to recognise and utilise the power of mathematics in solving problems and to develop their own mathematical thinking. (DES and Welsh Office, 1989, p. D4)

Scottish Guidelines highlight the need for pupils to:

work with patterns and sequences ... recognize and explain simple relationships ... use notation to describe general relationships ... use and devise simple rules. (SOED, 1991, p. 33)

The references that have been incorporated in this chapter indicate the relevance internationally of the subject matter included in this book and the many parallels that exist between nations and across the developed world.

REFERENCES

DES and Welsh Office (1989) *Mathematics in the National Curriculum – Non-Statutory Guidance.* London: HMSO.

NCTM (National Council of Teachers of Mathematics) (1989) *USA Curriculum and Evaluation Standards for School Mathematics.* Reston, VA: NCTM.

SCAA (School Curriculum and Assessment Authority) (1994) *Mathematics in the National Curriculum for England and Wales (Draft Proposals).* London: HMSO.

SOED (Scottish Office Education Department) (1991) *Curriculum and Assessment in Scotland National Guidelines: Mathematics 5–14.* Edinburgh: SOED.

CHAPTER 1

Focus on Thinking

JULIA ANGHILERI

Meeting the needs of a changing society

Anyone who has the opportunity to compare the types of mathematics books that were used by our grandparents with those found in school today cannot fail to be impressed by the changes that have taken place. Not only are there colourful illustrations and attractive covers but the content is starkly different. The page after page of 'sums' of ever-increasing difficulty that were so familiar to previous generations have been replaced with a variety of tasks and investigations to entice children into the fascinating world of mathematics today. The illustrations suggest that mathematics is relevant to the ways in which we live: designing car parks, researching market trends and exploring strategies for games are all examples of the applications for mathematics that may be found in children's texts. Geometry and arithmetic will inevitably be included as the 'backbone' to mathematics but exercises may suggest activities with calculators or computers to explore numbers and shapes in ways that will be relevant in tomorrow's world.

At first, the modern books may look easy, but closer scrutiny will show that the demands made on children are based on understanding and original thinking rather than the replication of skills to be applied in standard procedures. Our grandparents were 'told' what to do and how to do it so that they could repeatedly practice standard methods like multiplying and dividing fractions and long division. They learned by rote their number facts and everyone was expected to use the same written format for recording work.

At the time, this was important because all important calculations were undertaken by people who shared common methods to enable transfer and communication. Businesses would have departments of human calculators working on the accounts and in daily life people would be familiar with the methods used by such people as shopkeepers to calculate change or to keep the records of sales and receipts.

Today, the business world and daily life would probably collapse if

1

computers and calculators were not available. Machines are used to weigh and measure, to design and to calculate, even to tell us the change we must receive when we are shopping. Now, the mathematicians are able to focus on planning and predicting, using powerful aids to assist with the laborious aspects of calculations and enabling them to consider extensive and complex problems. Children in school today will be the users of mathematics in the twenty-first century and their skills must address the needs of everyday living in the society of the future.

It is crucial to develop in children the ability to tackle problems with initiative and confidence. The emphasis for school mathematics has changed from careful rehearsal of standard procedures to a focus on mathematical thinking and communication to prepare them for the world of tomorrow. Outlining a 'New Vision of School Mathematics', the USA National Council for Teachers of Mathematics (1989) note that

> knowing mathematics means being able to use it in purposeful ways. To learn mathematics, students must be engaged in exploring, conjecturing, and thinking rather than in rote learning of rules and procedures ... [to] make sense of mathematics [students need to] view and use it as a tool for reasoning and problem solving. (NCTM, 1989, p. 5)

This view is echoed in the *National Curriculum for Mathematics for England and Wales* (DES, 1991) where 'Using and Applying Mathematics' is one of the four Attainment Targets requiring that:

> Pupils should choose and make use of knowledge, skills and understanding outlined in the programmes of study in practical tasks, in real-life problems and to investigate within mathematics itself. (DES, 1991, p. 1)

It is also specific in the *Scottish National Guidelines: Mathematics 5–14* (1991) where the listed aims of mathematics are:

- to understand the nature and purpose of mathematics;
- to acquire skills in mathematical thinking with a supporting network of concepts, facts and techniques;
- to develop confidence in using and applying mathematics and to learn to enjoy its challenges and aesthetic satisfactions. (SOED, 1991, p. 5)

2

Theories of learning

If we investigate the reasons for change in school mathematics, we will find that they not only reflect the changing needs of society and the development of technical aids but also the work of psychologists researching the ways in which children learn mathematics. Early in this century, the dominant theory of learning was described as 'behaviourist' and was based on experiments to discover the way animals behaved and 'learned'. The behaviourist approach relied upon the notion that all human learning and behaviour was explainable as a response to external stimuli. It was believed that knowledge could be 'transferred' from a teacher to the children in class and that 'drill and practice' was the way in which children acquired such knowledge. Where children were able to make connections in the mathematical knowledge they were acquiring, this provided the basis for further learning. Where facts and techniques were learned in isolation, the result was often an overload on memory, resulting in half remembered rules and confusion. Ask any adult how to divide fractions (e.g. $\frac{3}{4} \div \frac{1}{2}$) or find the square root of a number (e.g. $\sqrt{574}$) and you will find few who can remember the rules they once learned. Even rarer are those adults who can explain why such rules work.

It was the evident shortcomings of the behaviourist theory that led to its being questioned as the relevant theory of learning for children as well as animals. While behaviourism might have been a good explanation of how to go about training pigeons to play ping-pong, it was inadequate when explaining the way in which human children learn to use language, to have ideas, to be creative and to solve all kinds of problems.

More recent theories of how children learn mathematics have come to be termed 'constructivist' and are based on the view that learning is not simply a case of 'transmitting' knowledge from one person to another but that children are actively engaged in constructing their own knowledge from their personal experiences. Mathematical knowledge is not something that is acquired by listening to teachers and reading textbooks but something that learners themselves construct by seeking out meanings and making mental connections in an active manner. It is the view of the constructivists that the learning outcome of any activity may vary from child to child according to the framework for understanding that each child has developed and that

3

the teacher's role is to provide an environment that stimulates active participation.

The life's work of Jean Piaget was devoted to the exploration of children as active constructors of their own understandings through processes he named '*assimilation*' and '*accommodation*'. As children interact with their environments, seeing, listening and touching things, they make sense of their experiences by relating new phenomena to those they already know. In this way they develop understanding and acquire knowledge as an internalized structure of their thinking (Piaget, 1964). This has been an enormously significant idea within the development of our understandings about children as learners, and Piaget has had an important impact upon modern educational approaches. Piaget's theory leads us to consider children as problem solvers seeking to make logical connections among the experiences they reflect upon. He proposed that children learn through a process of 'active self-discovery' while they are engaged in manipulating the physical environment, and this means that it is important for them to create and observe situations for themselves rather than being told facts and rules. He stresses the importance of activity in children's learning and his theories have led to widespread use of manipulative materials in the classroom and focus on problem solving as the basis for learning mathematics rather than the repetition of abstract taught procedures.

Although there are aspects of his theory that have been questioned, for example the close association he proposed between age and types of 'logico-mathematical thinking' and his lack of consideration of the social and environmental influences on learning, his work has had enormous impact on the way children are taught. For the reader who is interested in researching further the influence that Piaget's theory has had on school mathematics there are many books available. David Wood (1988) provides an accessible account of how this theory relates to children's learning in his book *How Children Think and Learn* and this is recommended for the reader who is unfamiliar with this theory.

Sharing the view that children are active participants in the construction of their own knowledge, Jerome Bruner placed greater emphasis on the role of language, communication and instruction in the learning process (Bruner, 1966). Bruner argues that instruction is necessary if children's spontaneous activities are to be transformed into abstract, symbolic thinking and that representation and the development of language play a crucial role. He labels three modes of representation: *enactive* where the child can manipulate real materials to depict mathematical relationships like matching sets in a one-to-one correspondence, *iconic* when the child can work with drawings or pictures representing relationships, and *symbolic* where abstract symbols are understood to describe mathematical relationships. In noting the importance of instruction, Bruner sought to describe the different processes that are implicated in creative problem solving and noted the role played by schools in the development of both children's knowledge and in the way they learn.

Both Piaget and Bruner place emphasis on action and problem solving in learning and they both acknowledge the importance of representation for developing mathematical thinking. Children will only come to *understand* and generalize lessons about abstract mathematics if these are based on practical experiences and problem solving that have led to reflective thinking.

While Piaget mainly studied the child in isolation from the influences that may affect learning, Bruner focused more on instruction and communication in the development of knowledge. More recent researchers on the theory of learning have emphasized much more the role of language and the social context in which young children learn both within and outside school. In recent years much research has been inspired by the approach of the Russian psychologist, Lev Vygotsky, who argued that all learning is essentially social in origin and that children learn from their families, peers and adults generally, as well as learning with their teachers (Vygotsky, 1978). Like Bruner, Vygotsky placed *instruction* at the centre of human development and argues that the capacity to learn through instruction is a fundamental feature of human intelligence. When adults or more able peers help children to accomplish things they are unable to achieve alone, they are not only assisting in the development of knowledge but helping children in the process of how to learn.

Such research has indicated that children learn most effectively when they are engaged in 'dialogue' with adults, and also that children benefit in a number of ways by being required to collaborate with their peers (see, for example, Moll (1990) for a good collection of papers relating Vygotskian ideas to education).

Classroom approaches

Before arriving at school, children have acquired an enormous amount of knowledge and have developed the ability to observe, to analyse and to make connections in order to try and understand events that affect their lives. Each individual possesses a 'framework of concepts' that will support the learning that will continue both within school and outside. Mathematical concepts they will have started to establish include ideas about quantities, shapes and sizes as well as ideas about classifying, sequencing and making logical deductions. When children arrive at school, the organization for learning may contrast with previous experiences but it is the same child with the same learning skills that need to be nurtured and developed to promote confident and informed approaches to the mathematical problems that school and later life may present.

Every individual child is different both in the situations they have experienced and their way of interpreting such situations but they have all learned to communicate, to question and to think. Within the constructivist paradigm for learning mathematics, teachers will build on the understanding that each child possesses, developing the language and skills in communication whilst acknowledging that the learning outcome for any activity is not easy to predict. Adopting a 'spiral curriculum', children will visit and re-visit mathematical relationships in a variety of contexts and begin to use language, adapting and adopting new language and negotiate meanings that enable them to make sense of the words and symbols required for abstract mathematical thinking.

Where communication and thinking are the focus of mathematics learning, it is not appropriate to have children working always in silence on their own problems. They must learn to express their own thoughts and to listen to the thinking of others. Learning mathematics will take place as they relate new problems to those they have experienced in some sensory manner, visual, tactile or aural. Think for a moment about how you, the reader, would respond to the questions 'How do you ski?' or 'How do you bake a cake?'. (Shut your eyes and think for a few seconds!) Most people respond to these questions by mentally 'searching' for some experience that will help them to explain these activities. For those who have no first-hand experience, visual images from the television or packets of cake mix on a supermarket shelf may be the next best aid to a reasonable response. For those with first-hand experience, it is highly likely that the image of their own involvement in some previous experience will be pondered upon (and enjoyed) for a brief while. So children will address all new experiences and problems by relating back to past experiences that will help them to understand new phenomena and structure new relationships within their personal framework of knowledge.

The teachers' roles involve familiarizing themselves with what children already know and providing experiences and opportunities to extend and sometimes challenge existing understanding. Active participation in problem solving through practical tasks, pattern seeking and sharing understandings will enable children to make their own sense of the relationships that underlie all mathematical knowledge. Working together in groups, children will become involved in describing and listening, discussing and negotiating, planning and evaluating, all skills in problem solving that will be valued in society.

Children must become familiar with the aids for mathematics that are available, from technical measuring instruments like digital weighing scales and watches, to calculators and computers. Concrete apparatus like beads and cubes, balances and rulers, will still provide sound opportunities to handle and view the models that are the basis of mathematical relationships. These will be supplemented by tasks that are designed to support learning with the tools used by practising mathematicians.

Although there are still some people who feel that electronic calculators inhibit children's thinking by doing all the working out, there are many skills in using a calculator and many patterns and relationships to be explored in a meaningful way. Calculators provide a powerful personal tool for mathematics that is available to everyone for tackling problems they will meet. Children will need to learn how to use one, to input data and interpret results and to perform the complex operations of which calculators are capable. Calculators today are not simply adding machines but many have programming and memory facilities that can be used effectively for complex tasks. Children will need to master many skills in using calculators as they provide one of the most valuable aids to mathematical problem solving available today.

Where lists of figures need to be added, this is often best undertaken on a computer with a spreadsheet which not only enables analysis of patterns and relationships, but also cross-checks rows and columns, and rapidly enables any changes to be incorporated. A spreadsheet not only adds, it can undertake complex calculations with thousands of numbers and produce answers almost instantly. What skills are needed are those of analysing the task and 'designing' an appropriate spreadsheet by giving instructions about where figures will appear and what calculations will be undertaken. Children rapidly become familiar with procedures that can be used (sometimes more rapidly than their teachers!) and this calculating aid can be used to investigate number patterns and relationships to further enhance children's understanding.

Computers are accessible to all children and most classrooms now have at least one available at all times. Many children show great facility with computers when they are given the opportunity to explore and experiment with support from a knowledgeable adult. That is not to say that the inexperienced teacher need fear the apparent speed with which children are able to familiarize themselves with changing technology but teachers themselves must be prepared to experiment and learn with support from colleagues and through In-service Training.

Because of the changing technology and the developments that are available in the society in which we live, the skills in mathematics that children require will need to be regularly reviewed. There is no question that they must learn the same number facts that have always been learned in school, but the ways they come to know such facts and the ways their mathematics is used can be very much more exciting than the opportunities provided for our forefathers. The mathematics classroom of today can provide a stimulating environment for activities in which each individual's contributions are acknowledged and valued and learning is a collaborative activity rather than the acquisition of knowledge passed down from the teacher.

In planning for mathematics teaching, a range of activities and teaching styles will also enable individual pupils to develop personal qualities and to enjoy the sense of achievement success in mathematics will bring.

The personal qualities which pupils need to develop include:

- motivation and preparedness to tackle the unfamiliar and unknown – willingness to 'have a go';

- flexibility and creative thinking in overcoming difficulties and developing new approaches;
- perseverance, reliability and accuracy in working through a sequence of stages in an extended task;
- willingness to check, monitor and control their own work;
- independence of thought and action as well as the ability to cooperate within a group;
- systematic work habits.

(DES and Welsh Office, 1989, p. B10)

Clearly all these are of value not only in mathematics but across all curricular subjects and well beyond the classroom into the place of work and everyday living.

Fascination and enjoyment

Above everything else is the teacher's responsibility to nurture a positive attitude towards the subject of mathematics so that all children will have the confidence to tackle life's problems. All children, irrespective of their ability or social background can enjoy the stimulation and fascination of mathematical thinking as well as developing self-reliance when they apply the knowledge they have acquired. Pupils need to see mathematics as a process that they can be actively and creatively involved in rather than a body of knowledge that 'belongs' to some one else. This sense of ownership will encourage reflection on the experiences of life and fascination for the relationships that are mathematics.

The fascination for mathematics will not be the same for every individual. It may come from an appreciation of pattern, a feeling for the order or the power of mathematics or the aesthetic beauty of designs and their relevance to nature and to natural beauty. It may arise through the conciseness of symbolic representation and the ability of the human mind to tackle and resolve problems. Any teacher who has witnessed success in mathematical thinking will appreciate the enjoyment it can bring and the enthusiasm for further challenges, for the human mind has a thirst to understand. This is always evident in young children and that must be nurtured in the mathematics classroom.

9

REFERENCES

Bruner, J. (ed.) (1966) *Studies in Cognitive Growth.* New York: Wiley and Son.

DES and Welsh Office (1989) *Mathematics in the National Curriculum – Non-Statutory Guidance.* London: HMSO.

DES (1991) *Mathematics in the National Curriculum.* London: HMSO.

Moll, C. (ed.) (1990) *Vygotsky and Education.* Cambridge: Cambridge University Press.

NCTM (National Council for Teachers of Mathematics) (1989) *Executive Summary of NCTM Standards for School Mathematics.* Virginia: NCTM.

Piaget, J. (1964) 'Development and learning', in R. E. Ripple and V. N. Rockcastle (eds) *Piaget Rediscovered: Report of the Conference on Cognitive studies and Curriculum Development.* Ithaca: Cornell University.

SOED (Scottish Office Education Department) (1991) *Curriculum and Assessment in Scotland National Guidelines: Mathematics 5–14.* Edinburgh: SOED.

Vygotsky, L. S. (1978) *Mind in Society. The Development of Higher Psychological Processes.* Cambridge, MA: Harvard University Press.

Wood, D. (1988) *How Children Think and Learn.* Oxford: Basil Blackwell.

CHAPTER 2

Emergent Mathematics or How to Help Young Children Become Confident Mathematicians

DAVID WHITEBREAD

The difficulties and frustrations of mathematics teaching in schools are widely recognized. Far too many of our young children find learning mathematics in school difficult, lose their confidence in mathematics, and go on to join that large swathe of the adult population who panic at the first sight of numbers. This chapter reviews a dramatically different and new approach to teaching mathematics to young children which promises to eradicate many of these problems. This new approach grows out of exciting work by psychologists and others exploring the ways in which young children learn. In recent years teachers' thinking about the teaching of literacy has been revolutionized by these ideas and developed into a new approach encapsulated in the term 'emergent writing'. This chapter attempts to describe how these same ideas relate to the teaching of early numeracy and together suggest an approach which might be termed 'emergent mathematics'.

In relation to literacy, the 'emergent writing' approach encourages children to begin writing by playing with written symbols, inventing their own 'writing' and using it for their own purposes (notes, lists, thank you letters, diaries, etc.). The teacher models the writing process by engaging in writing for her own real purposes explicitly in the presence of the children. The children's writing is valued by the teacher; stories written, for example, might be 'published' in the form of books and placed alongside other books in the class reading corner. This approach to the written word represents an attempt to build on what children already know, and it appears to be very successful in classrooms where it has been implemented. In such classes children have been found to write much more, much earlier and with more meaning, confidence and enjoyment than children taught to write by more traditional methods (Hall, 1989).

Together with the written word, mathematics is a major symbol

11

system which young children need to understand. The 'emergent mathematics' approach recognizes that, as with writing, children need to develop an understanding of numbers by playing with them and using them for their own purposes. They need to talk about their mathematical ideas with other children and with teachers, begin by representing mathematical processes in ways which make sense to them, and become more aware of their teacher's, and their own mathematical thinking.

This chapter is divided into three sections. The first section presents an analysis of the nature of children's difficulties with school mathematics. The second section reviews recent findings from developmental psychology which have demonstrated some of the causes of these difficulties, and begun to indicate new ways of assisting children's learning. The final section examines practical implications of these new ideas for teaching mathematics to young children, and itemizes the essential elements of an 'emergent mathematics' approach.

Why do young children find school mathematics difficult?

When we are considering the difficulties young children have with mathematics it is important to draw a distinction between what we might call 'home' mathematics and 'school' mathematics. Home mathematics is learnt (rather than taught!) in real world contexts for real purposes. It invariably involves particular objects and is rarely, if ever, recorded. It involves such things as counting the number of stairs, playing snakes and ladders, handling pocket money and sharing out sweets. School mathematics, by contrast, is often carried out for its own sake, unrelated to any real or particular context, and almost always involves recording using written symbols. At home, children become very confident in relation to the kind of mathematical problems they come across, but that the story is very different with the type of mathematics they often face in school. Some important pointers towards making formal mathematics more accessible to young children can therefore be gained by examining the differences between these two contexts, and young children's responses to them.

Many primary school teachers over the last 20 or 30 years have been influenced in their approach to young children's mathematics by

Piaget (1952) whose work appeared to suggest that before young children arrived at school they had very little understanding of number. Researchers such as Gelman and Gallistel (1978) have demonstrated that pre-school children from as early as the age of two know a lot more about numbers than had previously been thought. Given more appropriate tasks than those designed by Piaget, pre-school children could demonstrate some understandings about counting and an ability to conserve number.

Studies of children and adults in developing countries, where they either have not been to school or have 'dropped out' early, have found that individuals who cannot cope with 'school mathematics' at all, can devise and perform sophisticated mathematical operations to solve real, everyday problems. Studies of Brazilian street children and other 'poorly educated' populations have revealed the ability to develop very effective mental calculation routines in relation to real and meaningful everyday practical situations. Brazilian street children trade at street markets from as young as 8 or 9 years of age. These children have been found to be capable of carrying out mental arithmetic calculations quickly and accurately. Learning 'pencil and paper' routines to solve exactly the same problems proves to be much more difficult, and might actually interfere with the children's abilities to solve problems (Nunes *et al.*, 1993, provides a useful review of work in this area).

If mathematical understandings seem to develop so easily and naturally out of school, why is it that young children often find learning mathematics in school so difficult? John Holt (1964), in his book *How Children Fail*, describes the bewilderment of young children when faced with school mathematics. This book is full of examples of children attempting to apply formal procedures they have been taught in school and getting into the most appalling muddles because they don't really understand what they are doing.

Subsequent work in Britain and in the United States has repeatedly confirmed this position. By the end of their primary schooling, the vast majority of children are capable of carrying out arithmetical calculations using pencil and paper methods they have been taught in school. Many of them, however, have a very poor understanding of what they are actually doing. In the UK, the Assessment of Performance Unit (APU), reporting in 1980, found considerable evidence of children's lack of understanding of the formal mathematical symbols which are the everyday currency of school mathematics. Children aged 11 to 13 years, for example, were presented with problems such as the following where they were asked to indicate the most appropriate calculation:

> The Green family have to drive 261 miles to get from London to Leeds. After driving 87 miles, they stop for lunch. How do you work out how far they still have to drive?
>
> | | | | |
> |---|---|---|---|
> | 87×3 | $261 + 87$ | $87 \div 261$ | $261 - 87$ |
> | 261×87 | $261 \div 87$ | $87 - 261$ | $87 + 174$ |

As many as 40 per cent of 12-year-olds were unable to select the correct answer ($261 - 87$).

In the United States, the National Association of Educational Progress surveys (NAEP, 1983) carried out in the 1970s and early 1980s, revealed a very similar picture. For example, 13-year-olds were asked to estimate the sum of $\frac{12}{13}$ and $\frac{7}{8}$ and say whether it would be about 1, 2, 19 or 21. Only 24 per cent chose the correct answer (2) while slightly larger percentages chose 19 (gained by adding the numerators, 12 and 7) and 21 (gained by adding the denominators, 13 and 8). Over half of the children thus produced ridiculous answers, presumably as a consequence of blindly applying half-remembered procedures for dealing with fractions of which they had no real understanding.

The problem of school mathematics as it has traditionally been taught is illustrated beautifully by an incident recounted to me by a mathematician colleague of mine at Homerton College, Alison Wood. This began with a conversation between Alison and her younger daughter Susannah, who was 7 years old at the time:

S: Mummy, set me some taking aways with carrying

A: How do you set them out?

S: You put T U at the top and then two numbers under one another, like this

Susannah
writes
$$
\begin{array}{r r}
T & U \\
4 & 2 \\
-2 & 7 \\
\hline
\\
\hline
\end{array}
$$

> **A:** Forty-two minus twenty-seven, how do you do it?
>
> **S:** No, four two take away two seven
>
> **A:** What do you mean?
>
> **S:** That's the sum
>
> **A:** But if you went along the street and saw a door with 42 on it, you wouldn't say, that's number: four two!
>
> **S:** No, of course you wouldn't, but that's nothing to do with it
>
> **A:** So what does it mean?
>
> **S:** Nothing, silly, it's a sum

By this stage, Susannah was beginning to get cross, and so Alison allowed her to finish demonstrating how she did the sum. She used decomposition and found the correct answer, which she read as 'one five', with no difficulty.

> **A:** Good, Susie, can you do forty-two minus twenty-seven?
>
> **S:** Fifteen
>
> **A:** Did you use the sum you have written down?
>
> **S:** No, I said, $27 + 3 = 30$, $30 + 10 = 40$, $40 + 2 = 42$, so I added 15 altogether in my head
>
> **A:** Look at the answer to the sum
>
> **S:** The numbers are the same BUT THE SUM IS DIFFERENT

Alison was then able to help Susannah discover, with the help of unifix cubes, why the two different sums produced the same answer. The mysterious and meaningless process of 'taking aways with carrying' thus began to be related by Susannah to real mathematics that she already understood, and thus dawned the possibility that school mathematics might mean something.

Not every child, however, is blessed with a mother who is a mathematician. One of Alison's colleagues at the time, David, also had a daughter in the same class, and she asked him to enquire about Anna's mathematics. A few days later he described a conversation he had with his daughter:

15

D: What sort of sums are you doing?

A: Taking aways

D: Show me one

A: T, U, four, two

    Anna writes   T U

                    4 2

    (She then crossed out the 4, replaced it by a 3 and changed the
2 to 12)

D: So where's the sum?

A: That's it

D: But why is it a taking away?

A: I took 1 from 4, silly!

D: I thought you put another number underneath like this

    David writes: T U

                      4 2

                −2 1

                ——————

A: Oh yes, we do

D: Can you do it?

    (She tries but fails because she doesn't need to borrow)

    She writes   T U

                  ^{3}4 ^{1}2

                −2 1

                ——————

                   111

                ——————

D: I don't think that's right, is it? How do you do them at school?

A: I ask Susannah

The nature and source of Anna and Susannah's failures of understanding are very typical. Their teacher has taught them a very clear and precise procedure for carrying out this particular kind of calculation, and both children would no doubt eventually master it. Their level of understanding of what it all means, however, is zero. The nature of the calculation required, or the instructions surrounding it, have only to be changed in the slightest degree and they are left completely stranded.

Four key features of school mathematics clearly emerge from this anecdote, and from the other more systematic kinds of evidence, each of which contribute to making school mathematics difficult for young children. First, it is commonly bereft of any real, meaningful or supporting context. In the words of one, often quoted, aspiring young mathematician, the trouble with mathematics is that 'it isn't about anything'. Second, school mathematics commonly involves the use of abstract symbolism. We will review below evidence which Martin Hughes, a British psychologist, has collected to suggest reasons why this should cause young children such difficulty. Third, school mathematics often requires children to use new 'pencil and paper' strategies which are not simply written versions of the mental strategies which they have already developed for themselves (compare Susannah's mental strategy for calculating $42 - 27$ with the written method she has been taught). Fourth, school mathematics is often taught as a set of prescribed procedures, without helping children really understand numbers and the ways they behave. There is often more emphasis placed on 'getting the right answer' than on understanding the processes involved.

It is important to recognize, however, that the answer to these difficulties cannot be to abandon completely the kind of mathematics that children learn in school. Formal mathematics may present certain difficulties to the learner, but these largely stem from features which make this kind of mathematics such a powerful analytic tool. Formal mathematics is a very significant human achievement which enables all kinds of complex and important problems and phenomena to be more accurately described and explored. Even in our everyday lives, particularly in technologically advanced societies, the ability to understand formal mathematical procedures is of enormous benefit, without which individuals are disadvantaged.

The argument of this chapter is that formal, 'school' mathematics can be learnt much more easily by young children than at present, if it is made meaningful from the beginning. If we are to achieve this, however, teaching methods need to be adapted towards an 'emergent mathematics' approach. This approach can be defined in relation to the four key features of school mathematics identified above. An 'emergent mathematics' approach involves placing tasks in meaningful contexts, helping children to understand the nature and purpose of mathematical symbols, encouraging children to develop and explore a variety of mental and written strategies, and requiring children to reflect upon mathematical processes.

These key elements of the 'emergent mathematics' approach will be further developed in the third and final section of this chapter. To get a thorough understanding of this approach, and the ways in which its key elements hang together, it is important to understand some recent work carried out by developmental psychologists. This work has revealed a number of important aspects of the ways in which young children think and learn which are of enormous significance to us as teachers. These recent findings underpin the 'emergent writing' and 'emergent mathematics' approach to teaching young children in these two most important areas. The next section reviews this work.

Psychological research: how do children think and learn?

As Julia Anghileri has reviewed in Chapter 1, there have been a number of different approaches to human learning, developed by psychologists. The dominant model in contemporary psychological research on human learning is of the child as an information processor attempting to make sense of, and derive meaning from, experience (i.e. to classify, categorize and order new information and to relate it to what is already known). This model characterizes the young child as actively processing information and generating predictions and hypotheses about their world which they are constantly testing against experience.

There are three main features of the human information processing system which are worth briefly reviewing. Each has very direct implications for introducing young children to the world of formal mathematics.

1) Learning by induction The first major feature of human learning which has strong implications for approaches to teaching young children is that it appears to be very predominantly a process of identifying patterns and regularities from the variety of our experience. As human beings we appear to be very able to engage in the process of **induction** (inferring general rules or patterns from a range of particular cases), but relatively less well-equipped for **deductive** reasoning (the opposite process of inferring particular cases from a general rule).

Inductive reasoning is the basic process whereby we make sense of our world, by classifying and categorizing experience into increasingly structured conceptual structures and models. The overwhelming significance of inductive processes for human learning has long been recognized, and has always been a strong element, for example, within intelligence tests. What is the next number in the sequence 1, 2, 4, 8, ? is a test of inductive reasoning.

By contrast, research involving syllogisms, for example, has consistently shown that humans have very real difficulties with deductive logic. The relative facility with which we all learnt the grammar of our first language, by working out the rules for ourselves (aided by a little 'motherese') as contrasted against the horrendous difficulty many experience attempting to learn the grammar of a second language by being taught the rules, and being asked to apply them, is a good example of the superiority of inductive processes.

This search for patterns and regularities within the variety of experience has important implications for the ways in which young children make sense of new experiences. They expect to find pattern and regularity, and they expect new experiences to fit together in some way with what they already know. This is the means by which any of us makes sense of anything new with which we are faced, by relating it to what we already know. This natural and powerful human way of learning is, of course, vastly inhibited when we are presented with new information or experience which does not relate at all to what we already know. This has clear and major implications for the ways we go about introducing young children to the formal rules and procedures of school mathematics. It is clear that tasks and procedures within school mathematics are often not placed in contexts which make them meaningful to young children. This is a point to which we will return.

2) Limited 'working memory' capacity The second major feature of human learning, which has strong implications for approaches to teaching young children, is that the human being is a limited capacity processor of information. Miller (1956), in his paper 'The magic number seven plus or minus two', demonstrated from a whole range of evidence that we can hold only about seven separate pieces of information in our short-term or 'working' memory. This is why as adults we can easily process in our heads a sum such as 17×9, but have much greater difficulty with 184×596. We know the procedures we must go through to get the answer to the second sum, and we can carry out each of the separate computations involved. What we cannot do is hold all of the information in our heads at once. While we are working out one part, the result of the previous computation is very likely to be forgotten. This happens all the time for children with much smaller numbers and less complicated procedures.

In order to cope with this structural limitation, a number of features of our information processing system develop. That each of these features are relatively underdeveloped in children is significant for their learning, and has implications for ways in which we can go about helping them to learn most effectively. I want to highlight three of these features in particular, which relate to the development of *selective attention*, *structured knowledge* and *processing strategies*.

SELECTIVE ATTENTION

To begin with, our processing is characterized by the development of ability to attend selectively to those features which are relevant to the task in hand. This is largely achieved by the processes of inductive reasoning discussed above, and is vital if we are not to be overwhelmed by the huge array of information which is bombarding us through our five senses every moment of our waking life. The commonly observed ability of children to notice and observe features of a situation or event which adults have missed or overlooked is just the positive side of their inability, through lack of experience, to attend selectively to relevant information. I well remember my own elder daughter's account of a machine she had been impressed by during a school visit to the Science Museum in London. From her description I guessed that what she had seen was a 'working model' of an internal combustion engine. When asked what she thought the machine did, however, she expressed the opinion that it had something to do with gravel, as it had been 'surrounded by the stuff!'.

Young children's inability to sort out the relevant from the irrelevant is a very significant feature of their early difficulties with school mathematics. Relevant features of situations or tasks are learnt by the processes of inductive reasoning. These processes depend upon the new task being presented within a variety of meaningful contexts (just as a new word or aspect of grammar might be 'presented' to a young child in their everyday experience of language). Often within school mathematics, quite the opposite has been the case with new tasks being presented in one particular way only, and divorced from any meaningful context. It is not surprising that Susannah, in our earlier example, had seen no connection between the 'home' and 'school' mathematics versions of subtraction, because the task had not been presented to her in a way which enabled her to relate it to anything she already knew. Often children taught to do sums vertically cannot do the same calculations when they are presented horizontally, and will say that sums cannot be done like that. They have not sorted out the relevant from the irrelevant because they have not been presented with the opportunity to do so.

Interestingly, much of the criticism of Piaget's work in relation to young children's mathematical understandings is concerned with the abstract and meaningless nature of his tasks. Margaret Donaldson (1978) and her collaborators reported a whole series of experiments which demonstrated that children often failed Piaget's tests, for example, number conservation, because they had been unable to sort out the relevant features of the task. Her book, *Children's Minds*, is an excellent introduction to the importance of meaningful contexts in young children's learning.

STRUCTURED KNOWLEDGE

A second feature of human processing which equips us to deal with the structural limitations of our memories concerns the way we store what we know. As we learn more about any particular topic, not only does our knowledge become more extensive, but it also becomes more structured. There are two aspects to this of which we need to be aware, namely *chunking* and *elaboration*.

Chunking is the process whereby several separate pieces of information become commonly associated, and so come to be remembered as one piece of information. Consider the following two sequences of nine numbers:

$$4\ 6\ 2\ 9\ 7\ 1\ 8\ 3\ 5$$
$$1\ 2\ 3\ 4\ 5\ 6\ 7\ 8\ 9$$

It is clear that as an adult the second sequence would be infinitely easier to remember, because it can be stored as one piece of information, i.e. the numbers from one to nine. For a child who could not count in sequence, however, both sets of numbers may be equally difficult to remember.

Elaboration refers to the process whereby as we become more experienced in an area, we make more connections between different parts of our knowledge. This has the consequence that we have much more chance to make connections with new information, to classify and categorize it, to make sense of it and understand its significance, and thus, once again, to select out the relevant features.

Both these features of the ways in which our memories develop are dependent upon processes of representation. This has been an enormously important area of investigation for developmental psychologists in recent years, and much research has been carried out to try to explore the ways in which our knowledge is represented and stored in our brains, and how these representations develop in children. There is still a great deal to be discovered about these processes but what is clear is that the ability of humans to use various kinds of symbolic representation, such as pictures, words, and numbers, is crucially important in the development of our cognitive abilities. This would appear to be because the use of such representation allows more extensive processing and manipulation of larger units of information.

In the 'nine glasses' experiment the developmental psychologist, Jerome Bruner (Bruner and Kenney, 1966, p. 156), demonstrated the power of one form of symbolic representation, namely language, as a 'tool of thought'. In this experiment young children were presented with nine glasses arranged in a pattern on a 3 × 3 matrix, thus:

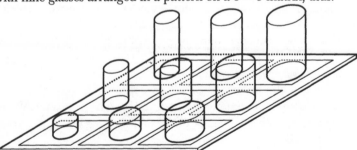

Figure 2.1 The Nine Glasses Problem (from Bruner & Kenney, 1966, p. 156).

The children were asked to describe the pattern. The nine glasses were then removed from the matrix and jumbled. The children were asked to replace them onto the matrix in the original pattern. The glasses were removed and jumbled again, but this time the bottom left glass in the original pattern was placed in the bottom right corner of the matrix, and the children were then asked to replace the glasses in a similar pattern to the original. Bruner discovered, very significantly, that while most of the children could reproduce the original pattern, there was a very close association between the ability to describe the original pattern by using words such as 'tall', 'wide', 'short', 'thin', etc., and the ability to produce the second, transformed pattern. He argued that the ability to process and transform information is dependent upon the ability to represent it symbolically.

The implications for teaching young children school mathematics are fundamental, and twofold. First, it is clearly important that they become confident users of mathematical symbols. If they are going to be of any use to young children, however, these symbols must be meaningful and integrated into their mathematical knowledge. As we shall see below, Martin Hughes (1986), in his research on children's understandings about numbers, has shown that mathematical symbols often carry very limited meaning for young children. Second, it is clear that young children need to learn to represent their mathematical understandings in language. The implications of both these aspects of the development of mathematical representation are discussed below. The encouragement of young children to represent actively their mathematical understandings to themselves and others is clearly fundamental to the 'emergent mathematics' approach.

PROCESSING STRATEGIES

The third major feature of human cognitive development, related to the need to work with our limited processing capacity, is the development of increasingly sophisticated intellectual strategies. These can be broadly categorized as general processing strategies, related to improving the efficiency with which the various parts of the human information processing system are used themselves, and domain-specific strategies, which relate to particular areas of knowledge.

Research has demonstrated that children appear to have very much the same processing capacities as adults, but they are very largely unstrategic in their use. For example, at the general processing level young children, relative to adults, search visual arrays for information less systematically, search their existing knowledge less thoroughly in order to make sense of new information or problems, are less likely to rehearse or categorize new information to help them remember it, and so on (see Siegler, 1991 or Meadows, 1993).

At the domain-specific level, in relation to mathematics, a lot of research has explored the way in which children gradually develop more sophisticated strategies, particularly in relation to counting and mental calculation. A number of researchers have looked at the emergence of the so-called MIN strategy for addition. At an early stage children faced with a problem like 3 + 9 will either count 3, or start at 3, and then count on 9. At some point, however, they realize that it is more efficient to always start from the larger number (i.e., start at 9 and count on 3). This is the MIN strategy.

The emergence of such strategies appears to be a very gradual process. Rather than just appearing out of the blue, new strategies are often extensions, modifications or combinations of existing strategies. After a new strategy has been used for the first time, an older simpler strategy is often reverted to for quite a while, and the new strategy only takes over very slowly. When faced with a more difficult problem, a simpler, more well-used, strategy often reappears. Children often appear to lack confidence in new strategies, and will double-check the results by using a simpler strategy. My own daughter, for example, frustrated me for years by insisting on counting out in 'ones' sums such as 23 + 10, even though she 'knew' (in some sense) that the answer must be 33. This issue of confidence appears to be crucial in this area. How we might go about helping children to develop confidently and explore a sophisticated range of strategies for dealing with numbers we will explore below. What is clear is that the present approach within school mathematics of ignoring strategies which children have already developed, and teaching them 'pencil and paper' strategies which bear no obvious relation to their existing strategies, is not helpful.

3) Developing 'meta-cognitive' awareness and control   After the dominance of learning by induction and the limited capacity of 'working memory', the third general feature of the human information processing system which we must consider is that it is a system which not only learns, but learns how to learn. The American psychologist John

Flavell (1981) was a prominent early investigator in this area. He pointed out that not only do individuals develop strategies, but they also develop the ability to use them appropriately. This is a consequence of what he termed 'meta-cognitive' processes, whereby we all become more aware of our own intellectual processes, and more in control of them. These meta-cognitive processes have been an area of enormous research effort within developmental psychology over the last 15–20 years.

Flavell and his collaborators carried out a series of experiments in the 1960s and 1970s which demonstrated the development of 'meta-memory' in young children. Children of different ages were shown sets of objects, and some of the objects were pointed to in sequence by the experimenter. After an interval of fifteen seconds, the children were asked to repeat the sequence. While 7-year-olds were perfectly capable of using a rehearsal strategy and remembering the sequence, 5-year-olds did not rehearse and failed in the memory task. When instructed to rehearse, however, the 5-year-olds turned out to be perfectly capable of doing so, and with consequent success in the task. But when the task was repeated, without the specific instruction to rehearse, many of the 5-year-olds reverted to not rehearsing, and failing to remember the sequence of objects. Flavell termed this failure to use an appropriate strategy, of which the 5-year-olds were clearly perfectly capable, a 'production deficit'.

Subsequent research in many areas of intellectual functioning has revealed exactly the same pattern. As adults we have learnt to monitor our own functioning very closely; we are usually aware when we do not understand something, when we have forgotten something, or when our current way of trying to tackle a problem is not working. Young children often show none of this self-awareness. Experiments carried out with the 'tip-of-the-tongue' phenomenon, for example, show that adults are very much more accurate than children in deciding whether they will recognize the name of something they have forgotten if they are told it.

As a consequence of this meta-cognitive monitoring, adults build up a store of knowledge about their own abilities and limitations, the characteristics of various tasks, and the potential uses of a wide range of strategies. Young children also show severe limitations in these areas. They are regularly, for example, wildly optimistic about the number of objects they will be able to remember when playing 'Kim's game' (where objects are shown briefly and then hidden under a cloth). Adults are generally very accurate with this kind of meta-cognitive knowledge.

The implications for children's learning of mathematics are clearly highly significant. As we have indicated within the earlier part of this chapter, and has often been noted by commentators, children's problems with school mathematics are not so much related to an inability to carry out taught routines or strategies, but more to their inability to be aware of when they are appropriate. How often have we all set children some 'problems', of the type:

Johnny has three apples. Timmy has four apples. How many apples do they have altogether?

only to be faced with the inevitable question:

Is it an add, Miss?

And this from children who could work out the answer to this kind of problem in their own way when they were several years younger. The teaching of 'pencil and paper' strategies for tackling certain kinds of mathematics problems is all too often done in a way which does not encourage children to reflect upon the processes involved, so that they can become in control of the new strategy. Sadly, all that often seems to be achieved, as has been found with such groups as the Brazilian street children, is to interfere with young children's natural problem solving abilities developed in more meaningful surroundings. It is clearly important within the 'emergent mathematics' approach that children are encouraged to be reflective about their own processing, and to adopt and develop strategies in ways which put them in control.

Implications for early mathematics teaching

The new understandings which derive from all this recent and current research into the processes by which children think and learn have clear and major implications for teaching mathematics to young children. To date, as we have reviewed, these new understandings have been taken on board most notably in the area of introducing young children to writing. What I wish to argue here is that the introduction of young children to formal, written mathematics would benefit enormously from the same kind of approach. In the final section of this chapter I want to develop and illustrate four key ideas or themes which together, in my view, define what is beginning to be called 'emergent mathematics'. This approach has been very much inspired by the work of Martin Hughes (1986).

Sue Atkinson (1992), in her book *Mathematics with Reason*, has provided an edited collection of classroom applications and examples of practice. In her introduction she defines 'mathematics with reason' by reference to fourteen points, from which I want to select nine which serve well as a definition of the 'emergent mathematics' approach (pp. 12–13):

- It is mathematics which starts from the secure 'home learning' established in the child before she comes to school
- It is mathematics based on understanding
- It puts great emphasis on the child's own methods of calculating and solving problems and rejects the previous practice of heavy emphasis on standard written algorithms
- Mathematics is regarded as a powerful tool for interpreting the world and therefore should be rooted in real experience across the whole curriculum ... Mathematics is brought out of the child's everyday situations
- Mathematics with reason is rooted in action – learning through doing
- Mathematics with reason puts less emphasis on representing numbers on paper as 'sums' and more emphasis on developing mental images in the child
- The main tool for child and teacher to employ in the mastery of mathematics concepts is language, not pencil and paper exercises from textbooks. The child is encouraged to talk about what she is doing
- Errors are accepted as an essential part of the learning process. The child, freed from the fear of criticism, will more readily experiment
- Mathematics with reason emphasises the thinking processes of mathematics, and these are made explicit in the conversations between adult and child.

In my view, these ideas can be encapsulated in four essential ideas or themes. As I shall attempt to illustrate, these derive directly from

27

what we now know about the development of children's thinking and learning, as outlined in the previous section. They also have clear and radical implications for our approach to introducing young children to the world of formal mathematics. These four themes involve *placing tasks in meaningful contexts, requiring children to make their own representations, encouraging and developing children's strategies,* and *employing a style of teaching which focuses on processes rather than products.*

Placing tasks in meaningful contexts

Most fundamentally, this new approach recognizes the lessons of research into 'home mathematics' and 'school mathematics'. Most children learn to understand and use some numbers with confidence and enthusiasm before they enter school. In real situations, where the mathematics serves real purposes, young children quickly and easily develop their own informal and largely effective methods. The difficulties start when they enter school and are expected to operate in the abstract, to use formal 'pencil and paper' routines and procedures and to do mathematics for no clear purpose. The example of Susannah and Anna's attempts with subtraction illustrate this point well.

Evidence about the way children learn would seem to suggest that what we need to do is to *start* with real problems, and work from them to abstract representations, not the other way around. As Margaret Donaldson's work has amply illustrated, placing tasks in meaningful contexts enables children to understand what it is that they are required to do. The point is illustrated well by Hughes' (1986) box game, which he reports in 'Children and Number'. Here, bricks are placed in a box and, as bricks are added or taken away, the child has to say how many bricks are now in the box. Hughes found that many young, even pre-school children were able to do this with small numbers, but they were completely flummoxed by being presented with the same sum in the abstract. Here is a typical piece of dialogue between Hughes and a 4-year-old, Amanda:

MH: How many is two and one? (Long pause. No response.)
Well how many bricks is two bricks and one brick?
Amanda: Three

> **MH:** Okay. So how many is two and one?
>
> **Amanda:** (Pause) Four (hesitantly) ?
>
> **MH:** How many is one brick and one more brick?
>
> **Amanda:** Two bricks
>
> **MH:** So, how many is one and one?
>
> **Amanda:** One, maybe.
>
> (Hughes, 1986, p. 46)

It is clear that when Amanda is faced with the real, concrete problems of numbers of bricks, she understands what is required and is able to carry out the calculation. She is able to produce some kind of internal representation of these real problems, and carry out in her head, perhaps by producing images of the real bricks in the box. The same problems posed in the abstract clearly fail to trigger the same kind of process.

There are, of course, abundant opportunities in the everyday activities of young children to get them involved in real mathematics. Playing games, sharing biscuits, deciding what is fair, finding out how many days it is to someone's birthday, cooking and shopping are all examples quoted by Atkinson (1992). In her book, teachers recount inspiring examples of exciting mathematics projects with titles such as 'Young children plan a picnic', 'Tracey and Jason make a map' and 'Children build a natural area and pond'. In one chapter, entitled 'Real "real problem-solving"' Owen Tregaskis argues that for problems to be real they must have direct relevance to the lives of the children. He describes a project in which his class planned, organized and ran a mini-sports day. This was done on their own initiative as their way of improving the school. They were involved in buying and selling refreshments, designing and making shields for prizes, and designing and running the various events (including marking out the running track).

With young children in particular (although this is certainly true throughout the primary range and probably beyond) problems can be real yet essentially born of the imagination. Problems arising through imaginative play or stories can often be even more vivid for young children than genuinely real life problems. A superb example of the possibilities of mathematics from imaginative play is to be found in the

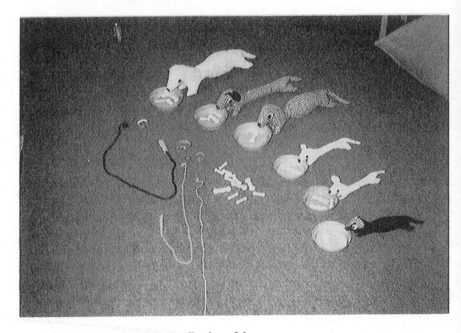

Figure 2.2 Zoe Evans' collection of dogs.

ideas and activities developed by Zoe Evans (see references). This British early years educator has developed a whole series of activities based upon structured collections of cuddly toys, including families of ladybirds, snakes and dogs. The toys vary in shape, size, texture, type of eyes or ears, etc. They also come with accessories like hats, bowls, collars and leads that invite matching and ordering activities that can be incorporated in stories and imaginative play.

These sets of animals are, of course, enormously appealing to young children, and each set has its own story to stimulate all kinds of sorting, matching, counting and other mathematical activities.

While young children may be helped to develop their mathematical abilities and understandings by tackling real problems placed within contexts which are meaningful to them, it is important, as we have stated earlier, that they learn to depend less upon the support of such contexts. Mathematics gains its power from its abstractness, and children need to be helped to become confident with abstract mathematical processes. The same process or concept needs to be presented to them in a variety of meaningful contexts. In this way, by the natural processes of induction which we have discussed, children are able to sort out the relevant from the irrelevant and they are ultimately able to abstract for themselves the essential elements of the process or concept.

Requiring children to make their own representations

The second element which is required to help children move towards abstract thinking in mathematics involves helping them to develop their representational abilities. This is my second key idea or theme within the 'emergent mathematics' approach.

Perhaps the newest element within the 'emergent mathematics' approach is the suggestion that children should be given opportunities to make their own representations of mathematics problems, processes and procedures before they are introduced to the conventional symbols. In this respect 'emergent mathematics' parallels very closely the ideas of 'emergent writing', where young pre-literate children are encouraged to make their own writing for their own purposes.

The significance of representational processes within the development of human knowledge and thinking has been indicated above in our review of the work of Bruner and others. Within mathematics it is clear that if children are to become able and confident mathematicians, they must be able to represent mathematics to themselves and to others, in language and in mathematical symbols. In this section I want to review briefly a range of work which has indicated, at least in broad terms, the kinds of ways that teachers can help children to develop these abilities.

That there is a problem in relation to children's understanding and confidence with the conventional mathematical symbolism is the central thesis of Hughes' (1986) book. He began by asking children aged 3 to 7 years to represent particular mathematical phenomena. For example, they were presented with paper and pencil, and a quantity of bricks was placed on the table in front of them. They were then asked:

Can you put something on the paper to show how many bricks are on the table? (Hughes, 1986, p. 55)

The children produced all kinds of responses which Hughes goes on to analyse. What he found to be highly significant, however, was that, despite the fact that the children from Year 1 onwards (5-year-olds) had mathematics workbooks full of the conventional symbols, it was not until Year 3 (7-year-olds) that these symbols became the predominant response. The children's lack of confidence with the symbols they had been taught in school was even more marked in relation to representing zero and the processes of addition and subtraction.

Intrigued by these findings, Hughes went on to invent the 'tins game' to explore children's ability to develop their own mathematical symbols. This game consisted of presenting young children (aged 4 to 5 years) with a number of tins, each of which held a different number of bricks, and asking the children to 'put something on the paper' on the top of each tin so that they would know how many bricks were inside.

Hughes found that not only could these young children make their own representations on the tins, but they were also very able to read these invented symbols back. Sue Atkinson (1992) has conducted similar experiments and has also found that children's own invented symbols hold enormous meaning for them. The conclusion that they both draw, paralleling the work which has been done with emergent writing, is that children gain an understanding and confidence in written symbols by first inventing and using their own.

Atkinson also provides a number of useful pointers to helping children make the transition from their own to the conventional symbol system. To begin with she notes that many teachers have found that children's development of the use of recording in mathematics is best sustained when they are allowed to record when they feel the need to do so. Processes of successive short handing and, interestingly, the use of calculators, both naturally lead children to introduce the conventional symbols into their recordings, in the same way that standard letters rapidly appear in children's emergent writing.

If children are to become confident and competent mathematicians, however, the development of written symbolism must be accompanied by the development of mathematical language. Indeed, many mathematics educators now believe that it is important that children express their mathematical thinking in language, through talk, before they begin to represent it on paper. James (1985) reviews the evidence of Bruner and others of the inter-relationships between language and thought, and propounds a mathematics teaching procedure which he terms 'do, talk and record'. This involves children in doing mathematics practically, and then following a five-step sequence of activities towards recording, thus:

- the learners explain their thinking to others;
- they demonstrate their mental images either with objects or by sketches;
- they record in writing the 'story' of what their sketches show;
- they make successive abbreviations of the process they used;
- finally, they can see the relevance of and adopt standard notations

(James, 1985, p. 43)

An enormous amount has been written about the need for young children to talk about mathematics with their teachers, and in groups with their peers. What I would like to do here, however, is briefly review some work of a student of mine which demonstrates a way in which teachers can use a certain kind of talk to help children develop representations of mathematical processes. This is an example of the way in which children's representational processes can be encouraged to help them to make the transition from context-bound to abstract understandings.

The student, Douglas Mayther, worked with 3- and 4-year-old children in a nursery school and adapted a procedure originally devised by Hughes (1986) once again involving tins and bricks. In the control group children were asked to do computations related to the number of bricks put in and taken out of the tin, and exactly the same computations presented as abstract verbal 'sums'. As Hughes reported, Douglas found that the children could tell you that there were two bricks in the tin, and when you had added one more there were three. But they were unable to respond at all to the question 'How many is two and one more?'

With a second group of children, however, Douglas carried out some versions of the task which appear to have helped the children to represent the problem to themselves in ways which facilitated the move from the concrete, real life situation to the abstract mathematics.

First of all, he used a tin without bricks and asked the hypothetical question:

If I put two bricks in the tin, how many would be in the tin?

Then:

If I put one more brick in the tin, how many would there be?

The next development was to use a hypothetical tin. With neither tin nor bricks in the child's vision, the same kinds of questions were asked again. These children were then finally also asked questions of the type 'How many is two and one more?'

Strikingly, many more were able to answer this kind of formal mathematical question. The procedure carried out by Douglas, he argues, required and enabled the children to internally represent the problem to themselves. This began with a specific image, in this case of a tin and some bricks, but the children were clearly able to use this to help themselves solve the more abstract (or, in Donaldson's words, 'disembedded') problems. This is related to the processes by which placing tasks in meaningful contexts help children to see what is relevant and irrelevant in a task, and which processes are required. Essentially, Douglas's technique appears to have helped children to provide their own meaningful representation of a disembedded piece of mathematics.

Given this kind of experience in a variety of contexts, the ability to make sense of abstract mathematics by reference to particular, concrete representations may well be encouraged to develop. As well as encouraging talk and make graphical representations, Hughes argues that children should be encouraged to use their fingers. These are, after all, almost universally the first symbols that we all use to represent mathematical quantities.

Encouraging and developing strategies

As well as being faced with abstract symbolism and new mathematical language, the child in making the transition from 'home' to 'school' mathematics is also faced with a range of new paper and pencil strategies. The difficulties this causes can be alleviated by new approaches to encouraging and developing children's strategies, and this is my third key theme within 'emergent mathematics'.

The new approach, as Atkinson (1992) reviewed, puts 'great

emphasis on the child's own methods of calculating and solving problems and rejects the previous practice of heavy emphasis on standard written algorithms'. As we have seen from the example with Susannah, and as researchers have found with unschooled children and adults, natural and informal methods of mental calculation are developed, and these often bear little obvious relation to written 'paper and pencil' methods. To take the example of the problem facing Susannah, many children and adults solve subtraction problems by counting on.

This lack of a relationship between informal and formal methods is a major cause of young children's loss of confidence with school mathematics. In line with other features of the approach, 'emergent mathematics' attempts to tackle this difficulty by recognizing the ways in which children learn new strategies, and devising a way forward which builds on these processes. Children need to be confident with new strategies, and this involves understanding how a new strategy relates to their existing strategies, and what are its appropriate uses. This can only be achieved by teachers first recognising the significance of children's existing strategies, allowing children to use them, devising ways of representing them (either verbally in discussion, and/or graphically on paper) and making it explicit that a range of strategies are acceptable, and all have their uses.

What is clear is that children cannot be encouraged to use new strategies very effectively by simply being taught them as an abstract procedure. It has long been accepted that children have great difficulty in using or applying the mathematical strategies and procedures they are taught in school. It is well-documented, for example, that children aged around 3 to 6 years are often capable of counting, and yet they fail to use this as a strategy for solving particular problems where it might be applied. A second student, Angela Root, recently carried out a study related to this particular 'production deficit'. This study very successfully illustrated one quite powerful way of encouraging young children to use a strategy by giving them confidence in it.

Angela identified children in this age range who could count a row of 9 beads, but used matching one-to-one rather than counting, when shown a row of 7 blue bears and asked to put out the same number of yellow bears. She then split these children into two groups. With the first group she instructed the children directly to use counting to solve the bears problem. The children were told to count how many blue bears were on the table and then to count out the same number of yellow bears. With the second group, Angela asked the children to set up the bears problem for her to solve. She then modelled how to use counting as a strategy for solving it, explicitly describing to the child what she was doing at each stage, and why.

All the children were then set a further bears problem of the same type, and were also posed a second, rather different problem. In this second problem, two rows of bears were set out on the table, a row of six red bears, and a row of seven green bears. The bears were placed in such a way so that the line of red bears was longer then the row of green bears, and the children were asked to say which row contained the biggest number of bears.

The results of this study were very interesting. On the original matching problem there was no significant difference between the direct instruction and modelling teaching styles. Both groups of children increased their use of counting as a strategy. However, the difference between the two teaching styles for the second problem comparing the rows of bears was quite dramatic. On this problem none of the children in the direct instruction group used counting (and nearly all of them failed to answer correctly), while around a half of the modelling group successfully solved the comparison problem by using counting.

This research has indicated that one way in which children can learn most effectively is when they are engaged in particular kinds of 'dialogue' with adults. As such, it is in line with the findings of quite a body of research which has been inspired by the approach of the Russian psychologist, Lev Vygotsky (see Moll, 1990), who argued that all learning is essentially social in origin. It is not difficult to see why the 'modelling' approach adopted by Angela might help young children develop a confidence and understanding with regard to a new strategy or way of proceeding. The children have seen that this is how an adult tackles the problem, and they have also been provided with an insight into the adult's thinking.

Employing a style of teaching which focuses on processes rather than products

This kind of research has also gone on to suggest that it is by such processes of social interaction and dialogue with more experienced learners (i.e., adults, or more experienced peers) that children learn to be reflective about their own processing and so begin to learn how to learn. This relates to the kinds of 'meta-cognitive' developments first identified by Flavell (1981) which we have reviewed above, and is my fourth key element within an 'emergent mathematics' approach.

All too often school mathematics is about getting the right answer, by whatever means. Many teachers have a wealth of stories of the ingenious ways young children have devised for getting the right answer without having to trouble themselves with understanding the mathematics. I once, for example, came across a child called Mark who was faced with this on a page of his mathematics book:

Making 7

7 + __ = 7	0 + __ = 7
6 + __ = 7	1 + __ = 7
5 + __ = 7	2 + __ = 7
4 + __ = 7	3 + __ = 7
3 + __ = 7	4 + __ = 7
2 + __ = 7	5 + __ = 7
1 + __ = 7	6 + __ = 7
0 + __ = 7	7 + __ = 7

'What's all this about?' I said.

'Oh, it's easy. I know how to do these', Mark replied, and proceeded to write in the numbers from 0 to 7 down the first column, and then again up the second column. The whole procedure took a few seconds. He proudly showed me how the same technique had worked for 6, 5, 4 and 3 on previous pages in his book, which were festooned with masses of lovely red ticks. It was not immediately obvious that he had appreciated the commutative law of addition (i.e., that 3 + 4 must be the same as 4 + 3), or that he was engaged in 'algebra', or that he had even noticed which numbers he was writing next to which, or even that there were addition sums on the page.

But he was getting them all right, and that was all that mattered. As far as I am aware, the teacher never saw how Mark completed these pages, and never discussed it with him. Since he was getting them all right, there was obviously no need!

It is the final key element in an 'emergent mathematics' approach, in my view, that processes must be more important than products. 'Mathematics with reason', as we noted Atkinson lists earlier, 'emphasises the thinking processes of mathematics, and these are made explicit in the conversations between adult and child.' (Atkinson, 1992, p. 13). Such explicit discussions about mathematical processes serve a number of important purposes. They clearly make it much more likely that children are going to develop understanding of the mathematics they are doing, and be enabled to make sense of it, and become more confident with it. They are the only clear way in which a teacher can reliably assess children's understanding, and become aware of the true nature of any misunderstandings, which must inform and vastly improve the effectiveness of subsequent teaching.

Finally, we have strong evidence that such conversations help children considerably to become more aware of and reflective about their own processing. The benefits in terms of helping children to become effective learners of this kind of approach have been well-demonstrated by such as Nisbet and Shucksmith (1986), who trailed a programme of meta-cognitive training for young children with primary school teachers and provide a useful review of work of this kind.

The development of meta-cognitive abilities may be fostered by 'dialogues' of a number of different kinds. As we mentioned above, one approach which a number of researchers have found useful involves an adult explicitly modelling and explaining a strategy in relation to a particular problem. Another approach is to encourage children to routinely question themselves about their understandings, and to reflect upon and record their achievements. Teachers can ask children to explain their approaches to problems, and discuss with groups different approaches to the same problem. James (1985) provides a range of examples of teachers talking to children about mathematics, and children talking to one another, in ways which are helpful in fostering these kinds of developments. He particularly singles out the value of children working collaboratively to solve mathematical problems. This obliges children to make their thinking explicit to others, and to reflect upon their own reasoning and choice of strategies and approach. One example he provides involves two children working out how much time each group of children can have on the class computer each day. They have to work it out together, and then show the class teacher the answer they have arrived at and, most importantly, they have to justify their method.

In summary

This chapter has attempted to describe what is potentially a very exciting and powerful set of ideas to guide the introduction of young children to formal 'school' mathematics. It would be arrogant and foolhardy to suggest that we yet know all the answers. What I hope is clear from this review is that, from the practical experience of mathematics educators, from research in children's mathematical understanding, and from the explorations of developmental psychologists related to children's learning, we do have some strong indications of the kinds of direction in which we ought to move. If we want to help many more young children make a confident start into the world of school mathematics, we need to:

- start with real problems, in order to present children with mathematical processes embedded in a variety of meaningful contexts;
- encourage children to represent their mathematical understandings both verbally and graphically, beginning with symbols of their own devising;
- allow and encourage children to develop their own mathematical strategies;
- involve children in a variety of kinds of dialogue which encourage awareness of and reflection upon mathematical processes.

As we have reviewed, the human information processing system has great strengths, but also inherent weaknesses. The current dominant methods of introducing young children to the world of abstract symbolic mathematics exposes the weaknesses of human learning. What we need to do is to harness its strengths. If we can begin to do this, the benefits for children's confidence and performance in mathematics will, I believe, be very remarkable.

REFERENCES

Atkinson, S. (ed.) (1992) *Mathematics with Reason*. London: Hodder and Stoughton.
Bruner, J. S. and Kenney, H. (1966) 'The development of the concepts of order and proportion in children' in J. S. Bruner *Studies in Cognitive Growth*. New York: Wiley.
Donaldson, M. (1978) *Children's Minds*. London: Fontana.

Evans, Z. booklets available from Hendre Craft, 'Old Barns', Newton St. Cyres, Exeter, EX5 5BY, UK.

Flavell, J. H. (1981) 'Cognitive monitoring', in W. P. Dickson (ed.) *Children's Oral Communication Skills*. New York: Academic Press.

Gelman, R. and Gallistel, C. R. (1978) *The Child's Understanding of Number*. Cambridge, MA: Harvard University Press.

Hall, N. (1989) *Writing with Reason*. London: Hodder and Stoughton.

Holt, J. (1964) *How Children Fail*. New York: Dell Publishing.

Hughes, M. (1986) *Children and Number*. Oxford: Basil Blackwell.

James, N. (1985) Learning mathematics, *Personality Development and Learning*, Unit 14, E206. Milton Keynes: Open University.

Meadows, S. (1993) *The Child as Thinker*. London: Routledge.

Miller, G. A. (1956) 'The magical number seven, plus or minus two: some limits on our capacity for processing information' *Psychological Review*, **63**, 81–97.

Moll, C. (ed.) (1990) *Vygotsky and Education*. Cambridge: Cambridge University Press.

NAEP (National Association of Educational Progress) (1983) *The Third National Mathematics Assessment: Results, trends and issues*. Denver: Educational Commission of the States.

Nisbet, J. and Shucksmith, J. (1986) *Learning Strategies*. London: Routledge and Kegan Paul.

Nunes, T., Schuemann, A. D. and Carraher, D. W. (1993) *Street Mathematics and School Mathematics*. Cambridge: Cambridge University Press.

Piaget, J. (1952) *The Child's Conception of Number*. New Jersey: Humanities Press and Routledge & Kegan Paul.

Siegler, R. S. (1991) *Children's Thinking*. Engelwood Cliffs, NJ: Prentice-Hall.

CHAPTER 3

Investigational Starting Points and Children's Thinking

DON MACKAY

The psychologist Jerome Bruner described three 'modes of representation' which children use to focus and communicate their thinking – the *enactive*, the *iconic* and the *symbolic* (Bruner 1966). The enactive mode involves real experiences and thinking by doing, the iconic mode involves signs, diagrams or perhaps objects like cubes or fingers to represent mathematical relationships, and the symbolic mode involves formal symbols such as numerals.

Many investigational tasks lead the child to recapitulate these three phases. A task is set which involves first acting out or doing something – the enactive. Children then represent this situation to themselves and others iconically, in the process shedding some of the irrelevant details of the real situation. Next by looking at the simplified iconic structure which has been created they are able to find a pattern which links with relationships already known in the symbolic world of formal mathematics. An example might be – enactive – build a series of staircases with cubes; iconic – record these using suitable diagrams; symbolic – find number patterns and make a general statement.

Teachers who are planning investigational work for the pupils in their classes might sometimes be pictured as going through the Bruner modes in reverse order. They have something mathematical or symbolic in mind towards which they want the pupils to work; they consider the kinds of iconic representations the pupils will need to produce to get through to the symbolic part and they devise a story or a practical situation from which the pupils can make a start. Teachers, in planning, attach the details of 'real life' which it is hoped the pupils will later discard in their progress back to the symbolic. For example the teacher wants her class to investigate square numbers; she thinks they could do this by drawing pictures of squares of different sizes on centimetre squared paper; she invents a story about a floor tiler who specializes in square courtyards.

Diagrammatically:

teacher wants pupils to explore	teacher considers	teacher plans/ pupil experiences	pupil explores	pupil discovers
↓	↓	↓	↓	↓
symbolic	iconic	enactive	iconic	symbolic

Finding the general within a maze of irrelevant detail has long been recognized as an essential mathematical competence. Zoltan Dienes described as one of four main competencies: 'The process of getting rid of irrelevancies and cutting through noise and getting down to the real message.' (Dienes, 1978). Richard Skemp also rates highly the ability to identify 'noise'. By noise he means 'data which is irrelevant to a particular communication' (Skemp, 1971).

In more recent work Valerie Walkerdine analyses pupils' mathematizing of situations within the framework of semiotics (Walkerdine, 1988). She describes pupils moving from the discursive practice of the story, or everyday life to the discursive practice of school mathematics via a chain of signification (i.e. the story is first represented by icons, then the icons are represented by the symbols of school mathematics). Importantly, she parts company with Dienes and Skemp in not seeing the 'noise' as irrelevant or trivial. She describes cases where the 'irrelevant detail' clings, colouring pupils' later thinking even when it appears to have been discarded, and claims that some children have to 'suppress' detail from one discursive practice in a psychologically complex process before they can enter the *school mathematics* discourse. This may occur because the meanings of the 'noise' bits within their everyday discourse is powerful and very different from the meanings assigned within the school context.

Choosing starting points for investigations

The project described below aimed to explore some of the effects of teacher-planned starting points by a comparative study of two investigations planned to lead to precisely the same symbolic point, where pupils would be able to use similar icons in their work, but starting from different enactive starting points. Questions in mind would be: to what extent would their investigative work follow a similar path? Would the detail of the starting point continue to determine pupils' thinking? Would pupils arrive at a common understanding at the end?

Would there be significant divergent sub-investigations which could be accounted for by the details of the starting point?

Two classes of 10- to 11-year-olds in Parkway Middle School, Suffolk were involved in the study. The outline of the project was to set two investigational tasks, one to each class, based on the Cartesian product aspect of multiplication. Here the Cartesian product refers to a product obtained by combining in turn the elements of one set with each of the elements of a second set. In the investigations in question, the two sets were to be equal in number, giving the following pattern where the number in the product is the number of lines joining the two sets:

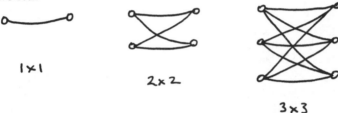

Figure 3.1   The Cartesian product aspect of multiplication.

Pupils who have learnt that a product means 'so many lots of something' can find the Cartesian product aspect of multiplication difficult with its combinations of elements which don't get multiplied in the normal sense of being reproduced several times. Hence it was thought an appropriate theme for investigative work.

The first class, Class A, began with a starting point about Henry's Snack Bar (hereafter called the Snackbar Task). Henry opens a Snackbar on a limited budget and at first serves just one meal, which is made up of one 'main' – cheese, and one 'filler' – baked potato. After several weeks of profit Henry was able to expand and provide two mains: cheese and burger – and two fillers – baked potato and mashed potato. Customers were served a healthy meal consisting of main plus filler, and could choose whichever combination they wanted. Later Henry added another main and another filler, then another, then another as his business flourished.

The second class, Class B, began with a starting point about a village being decorated with coloured lights for Christmas (the Lights Task). The main street of the village consists of two rows of houses opposite each other. The residents at No. 1 hang coloured lights across the street to No. 2 which is opposite. Then the residents at No. 3 do the same to No. 4. No. 1 also joins up to No. 4 and No. 2 joins up to No. 3, so that each of the houses is joined up to every house on the opposite side of the street. Then the process continues along the street.

Each of the tasks was introduced in the classroom in a way that encouraged pupils to start work in similar ways. Pupils were asked to stand out in rows to represent in one case the foods and in the other case the houses. Links were made between then using string, as shown in the diagram:

Figure 3.2   Using string to show links between two sets.

The two classes were thus brought to an equivalent point and an identical structure physically acted out in the classroom. From this point their own thinking and investigating took over. In both classes most of the pupils showed a tendency to discard some of the details during the course of their work in their representations of food choices and houses with cables of lights. In the Snackbar Task many pupils began with labelled diagrams of foods such as burgers, potatoes, etc., with some of these later using just words without pictures, and in some cases simple abstract shapes to represent the foods. In the Lights Task pupils often started with schematic pictures of houses having doors, windows, roofs and door numbers. The wires with light bulbs were shown as lines with light bulbs drawn on them. In subsequent diagrams many pupils changed to drawing a rectangle with or without a door number to represent a house. Wires were often subsequently shown as lines without attempts to represent the light bulbs.

The charts below show the extent to which the pupils discarded details in their diagrams as the investigation went on, suggesting strongly that their thinking at this stage was focused on the context of the problem rather than the mathematical implications. In Skemp's terms the focus at this stage seemed to be on identifying and getting rid of 'noise'.

SNACKBAR TASK

how foods are depicted	no. of pupils at start	no. of pupils later in task
drawings of foods	0	1
labelled drawings of foods	15	9
words for foods	10	12
abstract shapes for foods	0	3

LIGHTS TASK

how houses / lights are represented		
houses have doors, windows, roofs	9	4
houses are show as rectangles with roof and number	12	10
houses shown as rectangles with numbers	1	2
houses shown by a plain rectangle	0	6
cables with lights shown with light bulbs drawn	21	7
cables of lights shown as plain lines	1	15

Some of the reasons given by pupils for discarding details from their diagrams were:

Richard: It would have taken ages to draw all the light bulbs. It made it more simpler so you could do it easier and quicker.

Neil: It was easier to do. I got a bit confused when I put the numbers on. (He is talking about the numbers on houses.)

Gemma: It took too long to do the drawings and the words. I thought you didn't need the drawings. Like burger – you don't exactly need to draw a burger because people know what burgers look like.

Hannah: There were so many lines it was a muddle so I made it simpler.

These comments are representative of pupils in both groups; generally, reasons given for shedding detail in the course of the investigation were:

  i) economy of effort – easier to do
  ii) speed – quicker to do, enables you to get on faster
  iii) diagrams get muddled as bigger numbers are involved – there is a need to do something to make it clearer.

These reasons occurred among different pupils from each of the two groups. In general it appeared that the thinking behind discarding details from the starting points was to do with getting on quickly, not wasting effort, and avoiding confusing muddle in diagrams. Pupils did not describe being able to see that the details were not needed or being able to see a pattern that made the details irrelevant. However, pattern finding may have been implicit in their thinking as there was obviously some decision-making involved in knowing which details to discard – in no cases were there representations of the houses lost in favour of keeping the chimney pots, or drawings of food kept, but the links relating them to other foods discarded, as may have been the case with younger children. Many pupils (but not all) were at this stage engaged in 'getting down to the real message' but were apparently not able to articulate overtly mathematical reasons for their actions.

Abstracting from the task

One pupil's work – Gareth's – stood out from the rest of the class in the Snackbar Task. He had worked by a process of 'cutting through noise' to a final diagram which used abstract representations (see Figure 3.3a). His friend and collaborator Robert had a similar diagram but still included illustrations of the types of food involved (see Figure 3.3b).

The quality of Gareth's thoughts can perhaps be best shown by contrasting them with Robert's. I asked Robert why he had made the last two foods on each side of his diagram into circles instead of words.

Mains

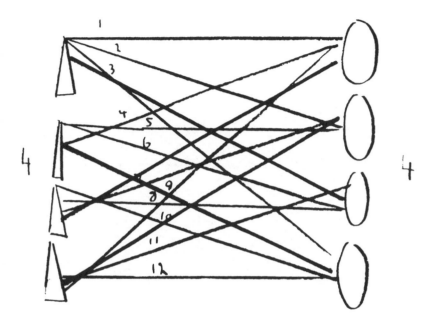

Figure 3.3a Gareth's representation of the Snackbar Task.

He said: 'To save time.' I asked him what the circles meant. He said: 'They're mains and fillers. The ones on this side are mains and the others are fillers.' 'But what actual food is this circle?' I asked, 'I know these ones – burger, beans, egg, because you've labelled them.' Robert replied: 'Any food. It doesn't matter as long as they're mains and fillers.'

Robert was using his diagram to represent some important general thinking. He had recognized that the actual foods are not important; all that matters is that there are a number of mains (in general) linked up with the same number of fillers (in general). Gareth spoke

47

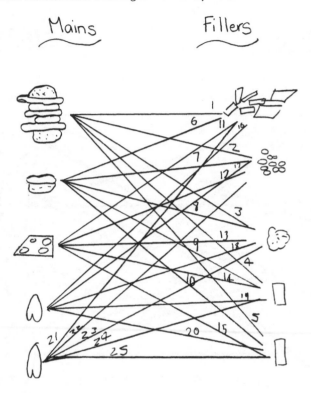

Figure 3.3b   Robert's representation of the Snackbar Task.

differently about his diagram. I said to him. 'This diagram is very interesting to me because there aren't any foods marked. What are these shapes?' Gareth said: 'Nothing really. I was thinking about this side going onto that side. I was thinking to join them up.' 'So they could be food or' 'They could be ... like pens on one side and pencils on the other side or something.' 'What would the diagram mean then?' 'Like ... what colours ... colour pencils and colour pens. Just join them up and that. What colour goes with what colour.'

Gareth, in contrast to Robert, is using his diagram to generalize from one physical situation to another. He has, in Dienes' phrase, 'cut through' the starting point and is able to construct an alternative enactive context matching with his diagram.

I found one other pupil, John, this time from the Lights Task class, who had reached a similar stage in his thinking. His diagram was similarly abstract, in this case with squares replacing Gareth's triangles and ovals. John discussed the meaning of these squares. 'They could be anything really. People walking from buses at the bus station or something. People walking to different buses. Buses on the other side. You come off a bus on this side, you go over to the other side to get your next bus.' As with Gareth, John is able to escape from the starting point and construct an alternative meaning for his icon.

Have Gareth and John reached the same point? There is perhaps one aspect in which the starting points still cling to their thinking. In the Snackbar Task the lines in the diagrams – the strings in the enacted starting point – represent combinations between two elements which can be chosen. Gareth's new idea retains this meaning. In the Lights Task the lines represent something in physical (spatial) reality – wires. John's new idea retains this spatial quality in the idea of paths followed by people changing buses. John is actually closer to crossing over to the combinations idea, and could perhaps with appropriate teacher questioning, see the alternative possibility of thinking combinatorially about his icon.

How did pupils make the move from diagrams to number patterns? This involves counting the links that go from each element. I tried to find out what led pupils to do the counting required in order to start to see pattern. Pupils were engaged in trying to find out how many links there were in total for a given number of elements on each side. One factor cited by several pupils which led them to start counting links from each element was the 'confusion factor'. With more than three elements on each side the muddle of lines made it difficult to count the lines themselves so they looked for a way to work it out. This often involved a strategy such as seeing how many lines go from each element on one side. Stephen said, 'If they're the same colour lines you wouldn't be able to see what they go to for a meal. It'd be a proper mix-up.'

Felt-tip pens also played an important part in many pupils' work. One strategy was to colour code lines leaving each element, to make them easier to distinguish from the general mass of lines. When this was done, the finished icon represented strikingly the fact that the same number of lines left each element.

Sam said, 'Well, the blue represents a baked potato on one list and the orange is mashed potato and the colours represent different kinds of meal or something. You count all the purple and all the green and you know how many you've got.'

Some pupils changed the colour of the lines at the midway point to show that the left-hand half belonged to the left-hand set of elements, and the right-hand half belonged to the right-hand set of elements. Neil said, 'I decided that if you timesed the amount on each house by the number of houses then you'd get the answer of how many cables of lights.' Stephen said, 'You could just count up three reds three blues and three greens. That's three threes – nine. That's the answer. Then its four lots of four colours.'

In general, when asked about how they found number patterns, pupils talked about needing to avoid confusion as diagrams got larger and more complex, and in other cases a colour coding procedure led to them noticing a pattern. In the case of the Snackbar Task, several pupils found an alternative way of representing choices. They wrote out lists of meals such as:

> burger and mash
> burger and chips
> burger and baked potatoes
> beans and mash ... etc.

I asked Hannah why she did this. 'If I did the diagram there are so many lines you can't see how many meals there are so I wrote them out so somebody who's reading it would understand it. If I just said there's 25 meals there I'd need proof to prove to the person who's reading it so that helped me to prove it. You've got to have proof because – if you say there's something like 25 they might not believe you.'

Hannah was more articulate than the other pupils who followed this strategy. From her account it seems that again avoiding confusion of a mass of lines prompted her to try a different kind of iconic representation – a list. She was also able to see the advantages of having a double-check on her results, in order to prove her results to a reader and to relate her solution back to the problem from which it arose. Her awareness of an audience is quite mature.

This use of lists to double-check and to prove did not occur in the other task at all apart from one pupil who began to build a colour coded key to the lines in the diagram:

(blue line) house No. 1 to house No. 2
(green line) house No. 3 to house No. 4

This shows the possibility of making a similar list but the context of combining elements in the Snackbar Task gives much stronger meaning to listing of pairs than in the Lights Task. As if in compensation, a group of pupils in the Lights Task class developed an extension to the main investigation which was not matched in the Snackbar Task. They began exploring spatial features of the linking lines. Several of them explored how many links there would be if you counted only the diagonal lines. Gemma also produced the following series of drawings which, although left without comment or explanation, nevertheless show insight into spatial qualities of the pattern made when there are three elements on each side:

Figure 3.4   Gemma's drawings showing the spatial features of linking lines.

It seems likely that the Lights Task class investigated spatial factors because in their case the lines in their diagrams represented real things in space. In the case of the Snackbar Task the lines represented abstract relationships.

Achieving some success

Comparison of the efforts of the lower achieving pupils was interesting. In the Snackbar Task class even lower achieving children succeeded in linking mains and fillers on a diagram for up to three elements on each side and then did counting to try to establish a number pattern, although not all succeeded. In the Lights Task class there were several lower achieving pupils who did not link up the houses with cables of lights as suggested in the starting point but made simple criss-cross patterns across the street. These pupils had difficulty in articulating why they made these patterns. A possible explanation is that they were trying to make a sensible pattern for cables of lights

51

hung across a real street. In other words they took the task at face value, rather than suspending disbelief and using knowledge about investigational formats to work out that the teacher was interested in patterns, rather than real cables of lights and real houses. From this point of view the patterns they made are much more appropriate for real light hanging than the 'right answer'. In this sense perhaps the first layer of noise that has to be cut through by the pupils consists of the conventions of school investigational mathematics.

Another factor in the relative success of lower achieving pupils in the Snackbar Task could well be the existence of a more imaginable outcome of the combinations – a meal on a plate. In the Lights Task there is no single object that represents the outcome of a Cartesian product. The outcome remains the series of links, in this case cables of lights.

Reflecting on the tasks

Pupils were able to pick up the investigation from each of the enactive starting points and work through often similar iconic representations to successfully discover number patterns and show these symbolically as planned by the teacher.

There were several ways in which the context of the starting point continued to determine the thinking of pupils even when general looking diagrams had been adopted. Abstract shapes in diagrams continued to be thought of by pupils as houses, or as 'mains' or 'fillers'. The more spatial Lights Task gave rise to spatial thinking amongst one group of pupils, where the less spatial Snackbar Task did not prompt such thinking. Even where very able pupils were able to generalize to other situations, the situations they cited were *combinatorial* or *spatial* in accordance with their respective starting points. In the Snackbar Task where the Cartesian product was a single real object – a meal – lower achieving pupils seemed to manage the task better than in the Lights Task where this was not the case and they reinterpreted the task in line with their less abstract view of the situation.

There was some evidence of the existence of 'chains of significa-tion' in the sense offered by Valerie Walkerdine. Pupils represented the enactive situation with icons and in doing so, in order to save time or reduce effort or avoid confusion, they decided to discard detail. This pushed them into making choices about what to leave out, and in some cases decisions about colour coding. The icons they created were looked at afresh and prompted insights and thinking not available from the enactive context; and these new thoughts were represented symbolically. Where an alternative way of representing the situation iconically (making lists of pairs) existed this opened up important possibilities for thinking about double-checking and later, proof, and for relating the solution back to the problem. This happened for one investigation but not the other, and could be an important point to consider in planning investigational work.

There was a wide divergence in outcomes of high and low achieving pupils. It is important to consider the richness of possibilities open to pupils of different talents who are able to get through different layers of noise in an investigation. This should be part of the natural divergence of outcomes. In one task (the Lights) there was resistance on the part of some pupils in moving away from a literally real-life conception of the situation, whereas the other task held more extended possibilities for pupils working in a literal mode. There should be possibilities for investigative work for pupils remaining throughout in the enactive mode.

A development of this work might be to help pupils to acquire a vocabulary to talk about discarding detail and cutting through noise which would enable them to articulate what they are doing more clearly than 'making it easier' or 'saving time and effort'. With higher achieving pupils sharing and discussing tasks done by different groups which converge on a similar symbolic endpoint might enhance their understanding of the power and value of generalizing. Making a generalization is perhaps too often seen as the endpoint rather than a powerful new place to start something new.

[Acknowledgements are due to Sue Neal and Lesley Farrow of Parkway Middle School for their help and their work with pupils.]

REFERENCES

Bruner, J. S. (ed.) (1966) *Studies in Cognitive Growth*. Wiley and Son: New York.

Dienes, Z. P. (1978) 'Learning mathematics' in G. T. Wain (ed.) *Mathematical Education*. Van Nostrand Reinhold Co.: Wokingham and New York.

Skemp, R. R. (1971) *The Psychology of Learning Mathematics*. Penguin Books: Harmondsworth.

Walkerdine, V. (1988) *The Mastery of Reason. Cognitive Development and the Production of Rationality*. Routledge: London.

CHAPTER 4

Between the Lines: The Languages of Mathematics

TIM ROWLAND

'Mathematics as communication' has become an explicit element of the school curriculum, and the society we live in – or at least a major sub-population – depends on people who are 'mathematically literate'. The workplace, in particular, reflects requirements that influence school mathematics today:

> A mathematically literate workforce is crucial because advancing methods of production make ever-higher demands on workers' knowledge and skills ... workers now must understand the complexities and technologies of communication and must be prepared to ask the right questions, assimilate new information, solve unfamiliar problems in unconventional ways, and work co-operatively as well as independently. (NCTM, 1989, p. 4)

Essential to communication is the confident use of language that is acquired through representing, talking, listening, writing and reading as children are actively involved in *doing* mathematics. But any discussion of the role of language in mathematics is complicated and potentially confused by the fact that the issue is so multifaceted. Among the considerations that are included in this chapter are:

- mathematics as a 'language', in the same way that Italian is a language;
- the interface between 'natural' language and the 'technical' language specific to mathematics;
- the form which mathematics takes when committed to paper (words, symbols and graphic material), and the way that learners interact with such text when they 'read' it;
- the language used in classrooms when teachers and children talk about mathematics;
- the private and social roles of language as a factor in the learning and teaching of mathematics.

These are not discrete areas, and I shall touch on most of them, for the learning of mathematics is an untidy business, however hard we try to tame and organise it.

Communication and ambiguity

It has been claimed that 'mathematics provides a means of communication which is powerful, concise and unambiguous' and that a 'principal reason' for teaching mathematics is the communicative power it provides for the learner (Cockcroft Report; DES, 1982).

On the other hand it may be argued that

> Everyday speech is a highly tolerant medium. This tolerance is necessary because conversation is a form of action in the word; ... Because it is a tolerant medium, everyday language is necessarily ambiguous.... Now, mathematising is also a form of action in the world. And its expressions, however carefully defined, have to retain a fundamental tolerance ... Because it is a tolerant medium, mathematics is also necessarily an ambiguous one. (ATM, 1980)

This claim is included in a pamphlet issued by the Association of Teachers of Mathematics in a section entitled 'Towards a language of struggle'. I believe this 'language of struggle' account to be a more resonant representation of the reality of mathematical communication in primary/elementary and secondary/high schools; and that the well-intended Cockcroft claim was in danger of reinforcing a public perception of mathematics as precise, logical, cold, austere and (for all except a 'clever' minority) unattainable. The claim is arguably true (or at least, mathematicians are obliged to proceed as if it were) only in respect as mathematics as a self-contained, written, symbolic form.

Thus the meaning of the (written) sentence $4 + 4 = 9 - 2$ is unambiguous, to the extent that the readers of this book will agree on what it asserts, and agree that it is false. This is possible because the definitions of the six distinct symbols in the sentence are known, agreed and very familiar. The sentence 'the sum of four and four is equal to the difference of nine and two' is less familiar, more impenetrable. Try it out in your classroom. I would argue that it is an elegant spoken equivalent of the earlier symbolic form, but how would you 'speak' it in classroom discourse? I shall pursue this question in more depth in a moment.

Shuard (1984) drew attention to the ambiguities and misunder-standings that arise from the fact that many words from 'ordinary' English have been adopted and given specialized meanings in math-ematics. Well-known examples include *difference, product, similar, face, volume, table*. I shall pause for a moment to consider one of these.

'Similar': Otterburn (1976) studied 15- to 16-year-old pupils' com-prehension of the mathematical language used in their public exam-ination course. One-fifth of the 15- to 16-year-old pupils in this study gave evidence of understanding the technical meaning of this word, which is arguably of less significance within elementary school math-ematics. It refers to a relationship between shapes, one of which is an enlarged version of the other. Thus a scale plan of the playground can be said to be *similar* (in a very particular sense) to the playground itself. In fact, children resort to 'the same' to make reference to a wide range of relationships between shapes (e.g. same number of sides, same shape and size but different position or orientation) including that of similarity. It is a challenging teaching task, and a valuable learning experience, to try to tease out what sort of sameness the child is (intuitively) aware of, and to encourage him or her to articulate it.

In a recent article (Jones, 1993) a Welsh-speaking teacher has drawn attention in a striking way to one effect of linguistic ambiguity. Jones analysed a sample of 224 examination scripts, half being English-medium papers and half Welsh-medium versions of the same paper. The two halves were matched samples, in the sense that the mean marks were virtually identical. However, there was a significant difference in performance on Question 12. This was a geometry question in four parts. Performance on the first three parts, which were about angles in three triangles, revealed little difference in facility between the two halves of the sample. However, the Welsh-medium candidates did on average twice as well as the English-medium on the fourth part, which began: 'Three triangles, similar to the triangles, ABC, JKL and PQR above, will fit together …'.

Now the Welsh word for similar is *cyflun*, a word which has no meaning in ordinary Welsh, and is used only in the mathematical sense, rather like the noun *tetrahedron* in English. Thus, Jones surmises, the Welsh-speaking candidates were alerted to a specific mathematical property of the triangles in the last part of the question, in relation to those in the earlier parts, whereas many English-medium candidates understood a vague 'sameness' relation which lacked the precision necessary for successful completion of the question. The examining board, understandably, had made no distinction between the candidates opting for the two versions of what, on the face of it, seemed to be the same mathematics.

Text conventions

In order to investigate such matters further, some groups of primary school teachers who came on a long In-Service course were asked to undertake a study of misunderstandings of this sort by close observation of three or four children working with some written text (usually the published maths scheme) whose mathematical conceptual content was judged appropriate for them. Having studied Shuard's book, they would make a pre-analysis of the text in an attempt to predict difficulties children might experience in determining the purpose and meaning of the text. Whilst the teachers were able to detect the obvious technical lexical hazards, and the crass results of carelessness or incompetence in the writing and publishing process (like a page about area in which every reference to a unit square was illustrated by an oblong!), they often failed to anticipate the way in which some children interpret some subtle text conventions. For example, the 'root and branch' form, as in the question.

> John has 24 sweets. How many will he keep if he shares them with
> a) 2 friends?   b) 3 friends?   c) 4 friends?

The responses: a) 12   b) 4   c) 1

are not uncommon, although these are not the intended 'right' answers. The problem here (if it is a problem) is that the response results from an intelligent, authentic and co-operative effort by the child to make sense of the task set out. If the answer is not the intended one (i.e. the one printed in the answer book) this cannot possibly be held to reflect on the child's mathematical competence. When a child gives a 'wrong' answer (i.e. not the one the teacher has in mind) it is always worthwhile trying to consider why s/he gave that answer. In consequence of our professionalism, we can often attempt to infer the reason (as in the sweet-sharing example above). If not, we can ask

'How did you get that?', which is one of the most useful, and under-used, questions in mathematics teaching. Incidentally, it is important to use it in response to 'right' answers as well as 'wrong' ones!

Commonsense versus logical language

These examples vividly illustrate the extent to which mathematics is, or may be viewed as, a language – complete with its own vocabulary, syntax and edifice of meaning. However – and this is at the heart of the ambiguity issue – the language of spoken (and most written) mathematics is always blended into a natural language (English, Welsh, French or whatever), and the distinction between the two languages is often blurred, sometimes deliberately so.

At the same time, mathematical language is embedded in the language of predicate logic, which includes such items as 'and', 'or', 'if … then', 'some', 'every' and so on. These too appear to belong to natural language, when they are in fact words borrowed from natural language and (in some cases) subtly redefined for logical purposes. By redefined, I mean that the ordinary commonsense meaning of some words is extended, (much as we extend naïve ideas of multiplication so as to include multiplication by three-quarters). Consequently, the range of permissible propositions becomes bizarre by conventional norms. For example, the sentence

'John is a boy or Mary is a girl'

feels like commonsense nonsense, yet we are obliged to entertain it (and consider it true) as a mathematical sentence. One reason for this is that its negation

'John is a girl and Mary is a boy'

is intuitively false. Similarly, commonsense offers no guide to the truth of the statement

'if daffodils are red then grass is green'

in that we are inclined to say that since daffodils are not red, the statement is silly, or even that it is false. On the other hand, formal logic judges it to be true, given our usual experiences of daffodils and grass.

Before leaving such matters, consider the question:

'Show that the sum of any two odd numbers is even'

and the response

'5 and 9 are two odd numbers, $5 + 9 = 14$, and 14 is even'

The fact is that the quantifier *any*, despite widespread use in mathematics at all levels, is irredeemably ambiguous, and may in turn be intended to mean *every* or (as interpreted in the response given above) *some*. For example, the question

'Is any rectangle a rhombus?'

can legitimately be answered both

'Yes, a square is'

and

'No, unless it happens to be a square'.

Many languages in one language

If we stop to analyse the range of skills which we use instinctively for everyday tasks, like tying shoelaces or riding a bicycle, we may wonder how we manage to do them at all. Yet anyone who has taught such skills to a child is forced to realize their complexity. Now consider the sentence

'A tetrahedron has four faces, any two of which meet along an edge'

which contains one or more examples of each of the following language categories:

(a) explicit logical language – *any* is an informal equivalent of the universal quantifier *every*;
(b) implicit logical language – the initial *A* may also be intended to have the force of *every*; the mid-sentence comma needs to be read as if it were the connective *and*;
(c) words such as *two* and *tetrahedron*, peculiar to the vocabulary of mathematics;
(d) words like *has* and *meet*, borrowed from natural language, which subtly personify the tetrahedron and its faces;

59

(e) words such as *face* borrowed from natural language and re-defined for mathematical purposes.

This analysis suggests that learning to *speak mathematics* is, in fact, more complex than learning to speak a foreign language in which, for the most part, the whole of the vocabulary is new. (However, there is a similar difficulty arising from the existence of *faux amis*; words (like *pain*) which have the same outward form in two languages (English and French in this case) but whose meanings are entirely different). In classroom mathematics, it seems to be possible to communicate a great deal without reference to technical language. Indeed, teachers may readily accept natural (or naive) language for the sake of communication and sustained confidence. Here I am talking to Susie, who was nine at the time.

Tim: What are you like at multiplication?'

Susie: What's that?

Tim: Um, times?

Susie: You mean so-and-so lots of so-and-so? That sort?

Tim: Yes, that's called multiplication. I'll say 'lots of'.

Susie: I'm trying to get divide and times together, 'cos I keep getting muddled up about what to do.

Tim: We'll try one. Suppose we have five lots of ... um ...

Susie: Fives is easy.

So it is substantially possible to 'speak mathematics' in a mode which has the surface appearance of natural language. It is hardly surprising that children may be unaware when natural language is being used for unnatural, mathematical purposes, nor that they are sometimes slow to acquire fluent use of the vocabulary and speech forms which are exclusive to mathematics. I survive holidays in Spain in just the same way. Hardcastle and Orton (1993) perceive a problem which needs to be tackled, and feel (emphasis added) that ways certainly do need to be found to *compel* pupils to use specialist vocabulary.

Nor is the problem peculiar to school children. Two days ago, in a supervision with an undergraduate student, it was painful (but, I judged, necessary) to witness her discomfort as she progressed from

I need to know if minus one is a ... you know ... I could use the thingy ...

to

I need to know if minus one is a quadratic residue modulo p. I could use the Legendre symbol.

Such moments are not a million miles away from a French conversation lesson. Learning to 'speak mathematics', is not simply a case of learning to use *jargon*. Rather, one is endeavouring to achieve fluency in a particular linguistic *register* (rather as teachers, firemen, lawyers and computer scientists each have their own register) for the sake of conceptual clarity and elegance of communication.

It is highly relevant, before leaving this section, to note the difficulties which are likely to be experienced by bilinguals learning mathematics in English-speaking classrooms. By a bilingual child, I mean one whose first language (that spoken at home, with his or her family) is not English but who can communicate effectively in spoken English (despite, perhaps, some grammatical irregularities). For such children, the fine nuances of word meaning referred to above will be even less evident, and much Eurocentric technical language (and perhaps, cognitive styles) of mathematics inevitably alien. The greatest danger is to assume that a child lacks ability on the evidence of what is, in effect, second language fluency in mathematics.

Meta-language: talking *about* mathematics

I want now to focus on language and thinking. First, it is useful to introduce a distinction between 'talking (or writing) mathematics' and 'talking *about* mathematics'. This can be illustrated by a short excerpt from classroom talk. Two girls, Runa and Kerry, are finding pairs of numbers whose sum is fourteen.

Runa: Let's put fourteen, and then.

Kerry: Right. Ten add four. Underneath.

Runa: Ten. OK?

Kerry: Ten add four, um, twelve add two, thirteen add one. [Pause] Um, nine add ...

Runa: Wait a minute.

Kerry: Five.

Kerry: Nine add five.

Runa: Yeah, I was just thinking that.

Kerry: Eight add six, seven add seven.

Runa: Wait a minute, is that right?

Kerry: You put seventy-six!

[they laugh]

This is what Runa wrote as they talked:

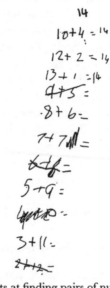

Figure 4.1 Runa's efforts at finding pairs of numbers to make fourteen.

Now remove the corresponding spoken words from the transcript:

Runa: Let's put [ ], and then ...

Kerry: Right. [ ] Underneath.

Runa: [ ]. OK.

Kerry: [ ] um [ ] [Pause] Um [ ] ...

Runa: Wait a minute.

Kerry: [ ]

Kerry: [ ]

Runa: Yeah, I was just thinking that.

Kerry: [ ]

Runa: Wait a minute, is that right?

Kerry: You put [ ]!

[they laugh]

What is left is a kind of commentary on the mathematics and the mathematical activity; it is talk *about* mathematics. Such natural language is meta-language relative to a given 'object' language – mathematics in this case. The distinction between the two language levels is disguised because, as we have already seen, mathematical language incorporates many words from natural language. The distinction is clearer when the object language is a foreign language, for example, when you arrive at the hotel, say 'Tengo una reserva', and collect your room key.

Now the meta-language of mathematical activity is not just an arbitrary and unimportant wrapping for the real business of doing mathematics. The way that teachers and children use meta-language can reveal a great deal. In the case of teachers, about their pedagogic style, because meta-comments of various sorts are central to the practice of teaching. In the case of children, their meta-language can reveal something of their beliefs and feelings relative to the mathematics they are engaged in. Such pointers to the status of their thinking in a social context are important guides to how we (teachers, part of that social context) can foster, refine and develop such thinking. To elaborate and substantiate these claims, I will be drawing on two aspects of natural language use in maths talk: the use of pronouns, and the use of 'hedges'.

Pronouns

It is fascinating to speculate on the attitudes and thought patterns which cause speakers to use pronouns in an irregular and almost interchangeable way, such as:

> When *I* got there [Oxford], *I* think the first thing *I* learned was that for the first time in *my* life *you* were totally divorced from *your* background. *You* go there as an individual. So what did *we* learn?' (*Margaret Thatcher, ITV interview, 29 March 1983*)

In Chapter 3 of his book *Speaking Mathematically*, David Pimm (1987) discusses the use of the pronoun *we* in adult social practice. Within a classroom excerpt, he cites the teacher who says (in the context of performing 26 − 17 in vertical form), 'What do we take from the tens column? We take a ten, don't we?'. It is a ritual intonement of a procedure (in this case, for subtraction by decomposition) which has been imposed on the audience, the child. This particular algorithm seems to be a particularly rich source of teacher 'we's. Shuard transcribed a similar conversation (given in full in Shuard, 1986) around the 'sum' 42 − 25, which includes:

Teacher: [...] Why can't you do it?

Pupil: Two ones.

Teacher: You've only got two ones haven't you? You haven't got enough. Do you remember, when we went through these sums last week, what we said you had to do, if you hadn't got enough?

Pupil: ... *err* ...

Teacher: What did we say you had to do?

It is inconceivable that the child is included in the 'we', forcing the conclusion that the teacher is associating herself with some other (unnamed) person or persons. Reflecting on data such as this, Pimm poses the question 'Who is "we"?'. He argues that the teacher, by using the plural pronominal form, is appealing to an unnamed 'expert' community to provide authority for the imposition of a certain kind of classroom practice. The effect is to discourage and devalue any sense that the child might make of the situation, and to urge acquisition of the 'proper way' of doing such 'sums'. Such appeals to the support and authority of unspecified others is not, of course, peculiar to mathematics. The linguist Dorothy David Wills (1977) observes that: ' "We" seems to have the greatest imprecision of referent of all English pronouns, and therefore is the most exploited for strategic ends'. John Major, in a speech (12th June 1991) to the right-wing Centre for Policy Studies asserted that: 'We have been engaged in the struggle to resist insidious attacks on literature and history in our schools.' Given Wills' observation, it is interesting to speculate whether Major was associating himself with the self-appointed Centre for Policy Studies, or with the elected government.

Caleb Gattegno, one of the founding fathers of the post-war re-appraisal of school mathematics, wrote in 1981: 'What is implied in the proper use of pronouns? Do children recognize them early and integrate them in their own speech with ease and total comprehension?' I believe that what Gattegno intended by this, in the context of mathematics education, becomes clearer by focusing on meta-language. I shall give some brief consideration to the pronoun *you* with this in mind. It is necessary to be able to develop some detachment from language patterns with which we are very familiar, in order to study them and to reflect on their implication for what teachers and children do in the classroom. As Paul Atkinson (1981) has put it:

> One has to work rather hard to make the effort of will and imagination to render what is familiar strange. One has to approach the data as if one were an anthropologist, confronted with a new, alien and exotic culture, and hence suspend one's common-sense, culturally given assumptions. That is what ethnomethodologists mean by the task of making everyday life 'anthropologically strange'. (Atkinson, 1981)

You can, of course, simply refer to the person or persons to whom one is speaking. The following such examples come from longer transcripts in Brissenden (1988), of two groups of children using a computer program, *Trains*:

Craig: Nine add seven, that's sixteen, it's one ten and six. [but he enters 6 first and then 1]

Steven: Craig, *you've* got sixty-one now, it's the wrong way round . . .

Gavin: Seventy-two plus seventy-two, that's a hundred and forty-four.

Teacher: Gavin, that was quick. How did *you* work it out?

In the extract which follows, I am talking to two girls about ways of 'making' twenty. Anna (aged 10) has proposed 'minus one add twenty-one'. In my 'bookend' questions, probing for Roksana's position, she is the referent of 'you'. But now study Anna's 'explanation speech', and consider who is 'you'?

Tim: Minus one add twenty-one. What do you think, Roksana? [pause]

Tim: Right, explain to us why that would give us twenty, Anna.

Anna: 'Cos nought add twenty equals twenty.

Tim: Right.

Anna: So if *you're* going into the minuses *you've* got to ... em ... *you've*, instead of saying twenty, that would equal nineteen, instead of twenty-one. And, minus, if *you're* doing minus ... one add, add minus one, something equals twenty, *you* go minus one add twenty equals, it equals nineteen. So *you* need to go minus one add twenty-one equals twenty.

Tim: Are you convinced by that, Roksana?

To some extent, our detachment, and hence our analytical powers, are limited by the very familiarity of phrases like 'you go' and similar. Heeding Atkinson's advice, try to take a fresh look at such uses of *you*, where the referent is not restricted to those participating in the conversation. An immediate response is that *you* is being deployed in place of the more formal pronoun 'one' (which, in fact, Atkinson chooses to use in the quotation given). In French, 'on' is more socially neutral. However, such an analysis of simple substitution obscures, I believe, the issue of ownership in relation to what is being asserted. The essential fact is that, in choosing 'you' in preference to 'I', the speaker has 'decentred' and become, in some sense, detached from what s/he is asserting. This could be for one of two reasons. It could be because of personal confidence in a claim or method that makes it available to others – indeed, to anyone. In the case of Anna, above, for example

'... *you* go minus one add twenty equals, it equals nineteen.'

It could be that she is sharing some kind of number line imagery that (she believes) should be accessible and convincing to others. By contrast, '*I* go' might suggest something idiosyncratic about her procedure. Here Susie, whom I mentioned earlier, is developing a highly idiosyncratic method of dividing 100 by various fractions.

Tim: OK. Now, you said that it wouldn't work for seven-ninths didn't you, this method. Right? Now, I'd just like you to write down five-sevenths, just here.

Susie: *I'm* going to have to think though, very well. Um, *I'll* try ... [pause]. Ahh, of course ... [interrupted]

Tim: You have a think while I push the door up.

Susie: ... *you* can't ... *I* don't understand. It's definitely a hundred. So that means two ... Ahh, ahhh [big moment] *you've* got two left, and *you* need five each time. So if *you* have two hundred ... um ... divided by five. How many times does five go into two hundred? Well, it goes into one hundred twenty times ...

Tim: Mm-hm.

Susie: Must go into forty times. So that's ... a hundred and forty.

Notice how, in Susie's penultimate contribution, 'I' becomes 'you' after the 'ahh' which signifies the moment of insight. This is one instance which illustrates a commonplace feature of indexical use (i.e. revealing personal characteristics of the user) of singular/plural first pronoun use. It is a striking and effective pointer to a quality of thinking.

Incidentally, in my 25,000 transcribed words of mathematical conversations with 9- to 11-year-old children, 'you' is the most frequently used word (744 occurrences), followed by 'and' (662), 'to' (400) and 'a' (394). In the 'dividing by fractions' conversation with Susie above (some 2200 words), Susie and I each use 'you' forty times. Every time I use the word, I am addressing Susie, whereas she uses 'you' to address me only twice.

On the whole, Susie reserves 'I' to mark her feelings and beliefs, or accounts of her personal actions, whereas 'you' indicates a kind of detachment from her strategy and computational methods. On the other hand, Anna's 'you' has some of the quality of the teacher's 'we'; it does seem to appeal to an unnamed authority of some sort, to support the method being offered. The distinction between the two girls is, of course, speculative, and based in part on evidence outside the scope of the evidence from the transcripts.

In his novel *Come home Charlie, and Face Them*, R F Delderfield (1969) gives this portrait of Evan Rhys-Jones, bank manager and landlord, described by his bank clerk and lodger, Charlie Pritchard:

He had ... a gravity that *you* could mistake for dignity until *you* adjusted to the maddening deliberation of his movements. It was this characteristic that fascinated *me* on that first occasion, so that *I* found *myself* wondering how long it would take him to select a stick of celery, bring it up to his chubby jaws and produce the soft, carefully modulated snap, in contrast to his wife's regular volleys from across the table. *You* had the feeling that if *you* asked him to pass the salt the meal would falter to an uncertain halt, so in the end *I* compromised, watching him but listening to his wife's coy exploration of *my* non-existent love-life. [emphasis added]

This alternation between first and second person pronouns, *I/me*, etc., and *you*, has the effect of distinguishing experiences and feelings from detached observation and objective comment. These two qualities co-exist in mathematical activity, and both are necessary. The meta-language can assist teachers to distinguish them in pupils.

But what are we to make of the teacher's meaning, in the Shuard transcript, when she says,

Why can't you do it? ... You've only got two ones haven't you? You haven't got enough. Do you remember, ... what we said you had to do, if you hadn't got enough?'
Whilst the 'you's could refer to the pupil, many of them could be interpreted as 'one', and convey the implicit message that 'we' have prescribed ways of doing 'sums' like these, and 'you' need to learn to do them, because, in the end, it's 'what *we* said *you* had to do. (Shuard, 1986 p. 90)

Even the pronoun *it* has a significant place in maths talk, acting on occasions as a pointer to concepts or generalizations for which the child has no name. I have developed this notion elsewhere (Rowland, 1992), using the data from my conversations with Susie. Aware that multiplication and division may 'undo' each other, she says, for example 'I want to know whether *it's* doing *it* or not' [writes $30 \div 5$] [pause] 'Six. And then six lots of five, five lots of six [writes $6 \times 5 = 30$]. *It* does work.'

This short study of pronouns gives a flavour of the potential of meta-language to reveal aspects of children's mathematical thinking which may be lost if one's attention is focused on the object language. As we saw at the beginning of this section, it tends to be the object language that is committed to paper. The only way in is to listen to children.

Hedges

A commonly-held view of mathematics is that it is about exactness, about right and wrong answers. Moreover the questions which teachers ask children are more often than not 'testing questions', to which they already know the answer. Such questions are deemed 'inappropriate' in linguistic conversational analysis, because they fail to meet the normal requirements of sincerity which are: that the speaker requires information, and has reason to believe that the hearer may be able to supply it. There is an inevitable asymmetry of power in teacher–student interaction, and mathematics teaching can be perceived as the effort to cause pupils to acquire some of the teacher's knowledge, to reproduce some of his or her behaviour. In such an environment (as to beliefs about what is required of teacher and pupils) there are intrinsic and extrinsic penalties associated with being wrong. There is insufficient acknowledgement by pupils and teachers that uncertainty is a valid, indeed an honest and honourable, state to be in. Yet such a cognitive state is to be expected when, for example, pupils are asked to make predictions and generalizations – features of learning based on investigation, enquiry, problem solving.

John Mason speaks and writes about the place of *conjecturing* in mathematical activity. Describing the qualities of what he calls a 'conjecturing atmosphere', he advises '... let it be the group task to encourage those who are *unsure* to be the ones to speak first ... so that ... every utterance is treated as a *modifiable conjecture!*' (Mason, 1988, p. 9 – his emphasis). Thus in the making and learning of mathematics, uncertainty is (or should be) expected, welcome and explicit.

Being strongly committed to the importance of conjecturing in mathematical activity, I set out to identify linguistic pointers to such a quality of thinking within transcriptions of interviews based on a task which I repeated with ten pairs of children aged 9 to 12. I call the task 'Make 10' because it begins with consideration of the number of ways that 10 can be 'made' as a sum of two 'numbers', and proceeds to similarly making other positive integers. (Extracts from 'Make 10' interviews with Runa and Kerry, Anna and Roksana, have already appeared in this chapter). The intention, as the task develops, is to provoke the children into making predictions about untried numbers, and conjectures about what might happen with 'any' number; in some cases to testing the generality of such conjectures, and trying to see why they might be true.

One striking feature of the transcripts is the use of words like: 'about', 'around', 'maybe', 'think', 'normally', 'suppose', (not) 'sure', (not) 'exactly'. Such words (called *hedges*) convey a sense of uncertainty – a state which, as I have already noted, one would expect to prevail in a conjecturing moment. The following examples are drawn from one interview, that with two girls, Frances and Ishka, both about $10\frac{1}{2}$ years old. At this point, having considered 10, 20, 13 and 30, they are invited to predict the number of ways of making 100 as a sum of two numbers.

Frances: Fifty?

Ishka: *About* fifty, yeah.

Tim: About fifty [. . .] do you really think it is fifty?

Ishka: Well, *maybe not exactly*, but it's *around fifty basically*? [. . .]

Frances: *Maybe around fifty.*

The linguist George Lakoff (1972) coined the term 'a hedge' for a word or phrase that makes a proposition 'fuzzy' (as Lakoff puts it) or vague in some way. I have discovered a great deal of interest in the way hedges are deployed by speakers (both teachers and students) in mathematical discourse, the goals they achieve by using them, and how they succeed in conveying information about the thinking of the speaker. The short extract above is chosen for the dense concentration of hedges which it contains (arguably including the rising intonation on Frances' 'Fifty?', indicating her lack of full commitment to her prediction).

There are (in speech and writing in general) two different kinds of hedges called *shields* and *approximators*. To see how they differ take, for example, an unqualified proposition P:

[P]: The next bus leaves at 3.15.

Now consider two possible ways (P1, P2) of qualifying it, i.e. making it fuzzy.

[P1]: *I think* the next bus leaves at 3.15.
[P2]: The next bus leaves at *about* 3.15.

SHIELDS: First examine P1, in which the hedge 'I think' lies outside the proposition P, which follows it and whose form is unchanged. The hedge is a meta-comment on P, and conveys the message that the speaker cannot be sure when the next bus leaves; perhaps s/he had been entrusted to find out, and had forgotten to do so. Such a hedge is called a *Shield* because it has a protective function. 'Plausibility Shields' like 'I think', 'maybe', 'probably', are frequently deployed by children talking about mathematics, i.e. in their meta-language. Here, we join Harry and Alan when they have found all the ways of making ten, and are about to be drawn into making a prediction about twenty:

Tim: So how many ways is it Alan?

Alan: Nine.

Tim: Nine, right. [pause] What if instead of saying two numbers adding up to ten I said two numbers adding up to twenty?

Harry: That would be about, yeah *I think* . . . that would be eighteen.

Alan: [simultaneous] . . . Eighteen ways. About eighteen *probably*.

Harry: No, *I think* nineteen.

Tim: Eighteen, nineteen?

Harry: I should write that again. [laughs]

Alan: What's that?

Harry: Up to twenty. [starts to write list].

I have invited the two boys to say how many ways there are of making twenty. They could list and count all the ways (many children did) as they had done for ten. Harry chooses to go for a prediction, to propose in effect a generalization, on the basis of the data that there are nine ways of making ten. Alan agrees; Harry instantly revises ('No, I think nineteen'), apparently rejecting a proportional rule (twice as many) in favour of an additive one (ten more).

The status of the prediction – a conjecture – is conveyed by the hedges, which Shield the boys from being 'wrong' until they are finally ready to commit themselves. When I seek the commitment ('Eighteen, nineteen?'), they decide to play safe and count!

Incidentally, teachers more often use 'attribution Shields' (distancing themselves from a proposition by attributing it to someone else) as a device not to 'close' on a problem, to sustain discussion and invite a variety of proposals, as in the example: *John says* you can't divide 14 by 3. What do other people think?

APPROXIMATORS: Returning again to the 3.15 bus: in P2, vagueness has been inserted ('at about 3.15') into the proposition P, by the inclusion of an *Approximator*-hedge 'about', thereby suggesting an interval of time of indeterminate length, centred at 3.15. The linguist Joanna Channell has done a lot of work on what hearers understand such vague quantities to include. Like Shields, Approximators such as 'about', 'around', 'approximately', as well as 'sort of', 'kind of', 'basically', can also have the effect of conveying uncertainty, as Alan does in the above extract; an unwillingness or inability to assert precise propositions or provide sufficient information.

The short extract with Frances and Ishka provides a rich source of Approximators 'about', 'around' and 'not exactly'. Their lack of certainty is conveyed in the hedged conjectures ('Fifty?'; 'About fifty'), but I press them to nail their colours to the mast ('do you really think it is fifty?'). Ishka responds with a masterpiece of multiple hedging, implicating in no uncertain terms that she is not yet ready to make the commitment that I seem to be wanting. The linguistic pointers are there for anyone whose ears have been sensitized.

In summary

Language is essential if teachers and students are to communicate and share mathematical ideas and beliefs. In our culture, an elaborate edifice of 'proper' mathematical language has evolved, which has an elegance and beauty of its own for individuals who have learned to speak and write it with confidence. But for the most part, in the teaching and learning of mathematics, the language of communication is a language of struggle, of compromise and negotiation. Students can fail to understand the meanings intended by teachers, because of the different language types to be found in mathematical speech and writing— Ordinary and Mathematical English, logical language, meta-language— which are rarely superficially evident. If we are at least aware of the ambiguities and misunderstandings inherent in classroom mathematical language, we are in a stronger position to diagnose learning difficulties whose cause may be linguistic.

The language and meta-language used by pupils as they respond to mathematical tasks is capable of conveying feelings, anxieties and degrees of commitment in subtle ways, including the use of hedges as shields against accusation of being wrong. These hedges may be recognized by sensitized teachers as subtle pointers to vulnerability in conjecturing activity.

REFERENCES

Atkinson, P. (1981) 'Inspecting classroom talk', in Adelman, C. (ed.) *Uttering, Muttering*. London: Grant McIntyre.

ATM (1980) *Language and Mathematics*. Nelson: Association of Teachers of Mathematics.

Brissenden, T. (1988) *Talking about Mathematics*. Oxford: Blackwell.

Delderfield R. F. (1969) *Come Home Charlie, and Face Them*. London: Hodder and Stoughton.

DES (1982) *Mathematics Counts*. London: HMSO.

Gattegno, C. (1981) 'Children and mathematics: a new appraisal', *Mathematics Teaching*. **94**, 5–7.

Hardcastle, L. and Orton, T. (1993) 'Do they know what we are talking about?', *Mathematics in School*. **22** (3), 12–14.

Jones, D. (1993) 'Words with a similar meaning' *Mathematics Teaching*. **145**, 14–15.

Lakoff, G. (1972) 'Hedges: a study in meaning criteria and the logic of fuzzy concepts', *Chicago Linguistic Society Paper*. Chicago: Chicago Linguistic Society.

Mason, J. (1988) *Learning and Doing Mathematics*. London: Macmillan.

NCTM, (1989) *Executive Summary of NCTM Standards for School Mathematics*, Virginia: NCTM.

Otterburn, M. K. and Nicholson, A. R. (1976) 'The language of CSE mathematics', *Mathematics in School*. **5** (5), 18–20.

Pimm, D. (1987) *Speaking Mathematically*. London: Routledge and Kegan Paul.

Shuard, H. (1986) *Primary Mathematics Today and Tomorrow*. York: Longmans.

Shuard, H. and Rothery, A. (1984) *Children Reading Mathematics*. London: John Murray.

Rowland, T. (1992) 'Pointing with pronouns', *For the Learning of Mathematics*, **12** (2), 44–8.

Wills, D. D. (1977) 'Participant deixis in English and baby talk', in C. E. Snow and C. A. Ferguson (eds.) *Talking to Children*. Cambridge: Cambridge University Press.

CHAPTER 5

Making Sense of Symbols

JULIA ANGHILERI

Understanding the symbols of mathematics gives the key to a powerful means of communication used abundantly in everyday life. Figures, symbols and graphs are used in all walks of life, for example, building, banking, journalism, advertising and politics and their use affects all members of society They are used to inform, to explain, to persuade and to assist decision-making for those who have the knowledge and confidence to interpret the information held within the symbols. This use and interpretation of the symbols of mathematics begins very early in school life with the symbols of arithmetic that provide the foundation for most of mathematics that is learned today. Starting with whole number sums like 3 × 4, and progressing to more complex calculations like 0.33 × 0.4 children are introduced to the language of mathematics that is to be interpreted and understood in its application to problem solving. But what does 0.33 × 0.4 *mean* and what pitfalls arise on the path to understanding this and other aspects of arithmetic learning?

This chapter will consider the role of the teacher in children's learning of arithmetic with a particular focus on the language of communication used in the classroom by teachers and by the children themselves. In it I will consider the symbols used in arithmetic and their interpretation as well as the use of words that are commonly associated with arithmetic operations. Detailed consideration will be given to the operations of multiplication and division which often present the first real stumbling block in arithmetic for pupils as they transfer from elementary to higher education. These and other considerations will help to identify the teacher's role in developing children's 'number sense'.

Teaching approaches

The mathematics classroom has changed from the days when the teacher *told* pupils what to do and how to do it, instructing them in standard procedures of the four *rules* of arithmetic to be memorized and practised, sometimes with minimal understanding and sometimes with no understanding at all, but learned by rote. Children are expected to be as competent in arithmetic as previous generations (as well as many new skills never learned by our parents!) but in today's classroom they are encouraged to develop their own methods for solving problems, to think for themselves and to communicate using language they understand.

In arithmetic today, children investigate relationships and develop number sense through practical tasks and real problems, relating their school mathematics to the experiences they learn from outside school.

> In order to progress ... pupils should be encouraged and helped to develop *their own* methods for doing calculations. As they develop in confidence and understanding, pupils will refine and develop their methods, building up a range of ways of tackling calculations. (DES and Welsh Office, 1989, p. E1)

This presents a challenge to mathematics teachers who must develop in children the ability to 'think mathematically' and to communicate both orally and in written and graphic forms in preparation for a role in the ever-changing technological society.

The change in teaching approaches, which is reflected in curricular guidelines across the developed world, has come about for two major reasons. First, the development of technical aids for calculations has had a profound effect on the society we live in. Today, most important calculations are undertaken with the aid of a calculator or computer and human calculators are no longer the valuable asset to business and industry that they once were. The emphasis of the mathematics curriculum in schools has changed to reflect the need for individuals who can understand and interpret arithmetic problems and their solution in a diversity of situations, rather than being proficient in some well-rehearsed standard calculation procedures.

> The K-4 curriculum should emphasize the development of children's mathematical thinking and reasoning abilities ... the curriculum must take seriously the goal of instilling in students a sense of confidence in their ability to think and communicate mathematically. (NCTM, 1989, p. 18)

Second, we now have better understanding of the way children learn.

Earlier this century, the process of learning arithmetic was based on the 'behaviourist' view of learning with 'drill and practice' instruction involving the repetition of standard pencil and paper procedures. Learning was to be thought of as a process by which pupils modify their internal models of mathematical matters in such a way as to mirror those which are held by their teachers. This 'transmission' model of communication is in contrast to more recent theories which suggest that rather than knowledge being 'transferred', pupils construct and modify *their own knowledge* in the light of experiences, both within school and outside. Following the work of Piaget, Bruner, Dienes and many others, teaching is being adapted to a 'constructivist' approach in which learners builds up their knowledge and capacity to think through active participation and personal understanding rather than being *told* by the teacher. These learning theories are discussed more fully in Chapter 1.

The role of language

The position and the role of language are summarized by one of the foremost proponents of 'constructivism', Ernst von Glasersfeld (1990) as:

> knowledge is the result of an individual subject's constructive activity ... language is not a means of transporting conceptual structures from teacher to student, but rather a means of interacting that allows the teacher here and there to constrain and thus to guide the cognitive construction of the student. (Von Glasersfeld, 1990, p. 37)

Building on 'constructivist' theories of learning, the mathematics teacher of today provides active experiences with opportunities for verbal expression in group discussions and in teacher–pupil exchanges. Pupils' use of language develops from naive everyday words and phrases to more formal mathematical terms and symbols expressing complex relationships with precision. By listening to children as they work on tasks, teachers are able to access individual's mathematical thinking and provide appropriate interactions to enhance and develop understanding.

Children's talk reflects some of their thinking but meanings are not always shared, either with their peers or with their teachers. In arithmetic, thinking involves words and symbols that can convey mathematical meaning in a concise and unambiguous manner but which may also sometimes cause confusion and conflict.

Symbols for words and words for symbols

If children are to understand the relationships that exist among numbers and the operations we use on numbers, it is crucial that they are able to understand what the teacher is saying and how this relates to the symbols they see on a page and use for calculations.

It is important to note that children's language often differs from that of the teacher, different words being used with a shared understanding or confusion arising from conflict in the use of particular terms. In addition, for example, children come to know that the symbol '+' may be read as 'and', 'add' or 'plus' and need to attach meanings to these words in order to solve written sums. Young children will get used to a particular word and parents and teachers will need to be aware of a particular understanding and be 'diplomatic' in expecting change and progression. Meanings need to be negotiated so that naive language that helps understanding can develop towards the more formal language that typifies mathematics.

Care must be taken so that this naive language does not inhibit progress to the more complex ideas that children will meet as they progress through their school years but children's perceptions need to be respected as the base upon which understanding can be built. By analysing the language associated with the symbols of arithmetic it is possible to identify aspects that may cause difficulties and to establish ways to build on informal understanding both in negotiating new meanings and in extending terminology.

It is well-known that the subtraction symbol '-' presents difficulties for children when it is used to represent the words 'take away' in some problems and the words 'difference between' in others. Consider the problems:

Alison had 12 marbles but she lost 3. How many marbles does Alison have now?
Alison is 12 years old and Aaron is 3 years old. What is the difference between their ages?

Both these problems may be represented as '12 − 3 = 9' but for many children the notion of 'take away' is not easily associated with the second. Where a child knows subtraction only as 'take away', confusion may arise in representing 'difference between' using exactly the same symbol. When asked 'what is the difference between 12 and 3?' a diversity of well-reasoned responses may be 'correct' in the eyes of children, including 'the first is an even number and the second is odd', 'the first has two digits and the second has one' and 'the first number has a one and the second does not'. The specific meaning given to 'difference' in arithmetic may conflict with the meaning of the word in everyday English. A discussion of this conflict between Mathematical English and Ordinary English may be found in Shuard's (1984) *Children Reading Mathematics*. Children must come to know that there are many meanings associated with the symbols of arithmetic and certain interpretations will match better the different contexts and different solution procedures that are appropriate.

The structure of both addition and subtraction and children's learning of these operations have been considered in detailed research, some of which is documented in Carpenter *et al.* (1982) *Addition and Subtraction: a Cognitive Perspective*. Such detailed studies analyse children's interpretations of tasks and propose stages in children's learning that inform teachers in a way which will enable them to support children's thinking. Listening to individual children and enabling them to develop their personal understanding become effective ways to develop confidence and avoid confusion that exists in much mathematics learning.

As children progress through their early years of schooling, the further operations of multiplication and division are introduced and need to be integrated into each individual's developing sense for numbers. By the age of 10 or 11, some children show sound understanding of the relationships involved while others begin to struggle and lose faith in their mathematical ability. Detailed analysis of some of the complexities inherent in the introduction of multiplication and division will help teachers to support and develop children's understanding. Language may be seen to play a crucial role as it increases in its complexity and diversity with subtle but crucial variations expressing the variety of relationships that are involved.

Language of multiplication and division

Let us consider in detail the operation of multiplication and its introduction in the classroom through repeated sets and repeated addition. Teachers and children will share the language of *sets of* or *lots of* as in *three sets of wheels* or more abstractly *three lots of four* (see Figure 5.1).

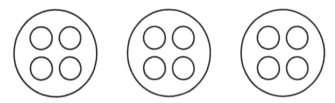

Figure 5.1 Three sets of four wheels – three lots of four.

This will be represented symbolically as 3(4) or as 4 × 3. Already we have a problem. Should we use the symbols 3 × 4 or 4 × 3 to represent this situation? This will depend on how we (teachers and children) are to read the symbols and needs to be negotiated from the outset. If we 'transfer' the meaning directly from the example above, the phrases '3 sets of 4' and '3 lots of 4' can be identified with the expression 3 × 4. If we take the more formal mathematical meaning that children are likely to meet later in their schooling, the phrase '3 multiplied by 4' will be interpreted literally as 'a set of 3 taken 4 times', i.e. four lots of three (see Figure 5.2).

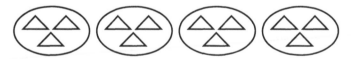

Figure 5.2 Three multiplied by four – a set of three taken four times.

Many adults and children use the expressions 'three times four' or 'three fours' to interpret the symbols 3 × 4 (Anghileri, 1990) and teachers must consider the experiences children will encounter outside the classroom in their developing understanding of arithmetic as well as the texts and examples they will meet in school. In an environment that is rich with language, children will come to know the meanings of individual words by hearing them and speaking them in meaningful contexts though it may take some considerable time before precise meanings are understood.

There is no easy answer to the dilemma that this presents. Considerations relating to mathematics words include the fact that *active* sentence constructions (e.g. Tom kicked the ball) are favoured by children over *passive* sentence constructions (e.g. the ball was kicked by Tom) and the phrase 'three times four' is attractive in its *active* construction when compared with the *passive* construction 'three multiplied by four'. 'Three lots of four' and 'three multiplied by four' may not correspond to the same visual images that children find so helpful in understanding arithmetic. Since each phrase corresponds to a different visual image (see Figures 5.1 and 5.2) it may be necessary to present to the child an unambiguous interpretation to avoid confusion or to acknowledge the dilemma and discuss its resolution with children and teachers.

It is sometimes claimed that 'three multiplied by four' is *mathematically correct* for it fits in with the other operations and the passive verbalization [the first number being 'acted upon' by the second] with which they may be associated:

$4 + 3$ – four add three – to four, three is added

$4 - 3$ – four subtract three – from four, three is subtracted

$24 \div 3$ – twenty-four divided by three

4×3 – four multiplied by three

It is certainly true that even mathematicians are inconsistent. I, like most mathematicians, am very happy to read the symbols 3×4 as 'three multiplied by four' or '4 lots of 3' but acknowledge the need to interpret symbols like 2n [$2 \times n$] as 'two times n' or '2 lots of n'. As an experienced adult, I can decide upon the interpretation that is appropriate to the situation involved. Some children may not have the experiences necessary to make such decisions and confusion may arise. Clearly this will not be true for all children and able individuals will often revel in their awareness that decisions are to be made – to realize that 4×15 is not only 15 lots of 4 but also 4 lots of 15 and even 15 doubled and doubled again, will give a sense of satisfaction and achievement to some children while others may struggle with $4 + 4 + 4 + 4 + 4 + \ldots + 4$, fifteen times.

When multiplication is 'extended' to include fractional or decimal numbers it becomes even more important to consider possible meanings of symbolic problems. The problem $4 \times \frac{3}{4}$ acquires totally different meanings when interpreted as 'four lots of three-quarters' or as 'three-quarters of 4' (note here that the phrase 'lots of' is adapted to 'of' in the fraction situation). The fact that each calculation will result in the same solution is certainly true but not self-evident and indeed may be very illusive for many children. The 'meaning' of '0.2×0.3' is not clear if the symbols are read as '0.2 lots of 0.3' or even '0.2 of 0.3' and substantial experience is required to identify what is *meant* by this problem at all. In this type of problem it is helpful to consider images or pictorial representations of multiplication perhaps using squared paper. Starting with the idea of '4×3' as a rectangular box, this image can be adapted to '$4 \times \frac{3}{4}$' and '$\frac{1}{2} \times \frac{3}{4}$' or to '$0.4 \times 0.3$'. Talking about these images will enable children to interpret in words the symbolic problems that they represent.

Teacher's role in establishing meanings

Teachers are sometimes unaware of the effect language may have on their pupils understanding of arithmetic. As well as 'giving' pupils interpretations of the mathematical symbols they will meet, it is important to listen to the children's own interpretations. As in any other subject to be encountered in school, there is the more sophisticated, formal language that the pupils will hear and interpret which may contrast with the more informal, intuitive language with which pupils will formulate their own thinking and discussions. Take a look at pupils own story writing in comparison to the books they may be reading. Children's sentences are simpler in their structure and the words used are often naive. If we use work created by the children as a reflection of their thinking, then we must match our expectations in mathematical language to the reality of their capabilities. This is not to say that formal language in mathematics is not to be used but that understanding of the meanings of words and symbols will develop, sometimes slowly, in line with pupils' experiences.

Naive versus formal language

When a new idea in mathematics is introduced in the classroom, there is strong justification for identifying understanding that the children may bring from previous experiences. The operation of division is a good example where most children will have experiences of *sharing* activities in the home or in school. Given a collection of objects (like marbles) or a single object (like a pizza) to share among a group, children will have strategies to allocate portions and use associated language about 'sharing', 'fairness' and 'equal portions'. These will form a basis from which the teachers may introduce division. If these naive ideas are not developed to incorporate the more formal language and broader meanings of the symbols they may inhibit progress when the division problems become more complex as illustrated in the following example:

Having successfully used the phrase 'shared by' to solve the problems

$$12 \div 3 \qquad 20 \div 4 \qquad 14 \div 7$$

Lorraine and Jody (age 11) spent a giggly five minutes contemplating the problem

$$6 \div \tfrac{1}{2}$$

Their conversation went as follows:

L: How can you share 6 with half a person?

J: You can't have that because you can't have half a person.

At this stage, Jody drew an illustration of a half-person to reinforce the impossibility of the problem.

L: I know! ... Half of 6 is 3

The idea of sharing relates to one of the interpretations of division and one of the solution procedures that may be implemented but does not relate to all division problems. Take, for example, the problem 'How many egg boxes can be filled with 18 eggs if 6 eggs go into each box?'. It is not a sharing procedure that is required but a 'repeated subtraction' or 'grouping' action that is needed to find a solution. Pupils cannot start with an unknown number of egg boxes into which they may share the eggs, they must start by removing sixes until no eggs remain. This problem will be represented in symbolic form by '18 ÷ 6' but cannot be interpreted as 18 'shared by' 6. Here some subtlety in the language may be relevant as the problem may be interpreted as '18 shared *into* sixes' and the notion of *sharing* takes on a new meaning.

Before written symbolic calculations in division are introduced, children will need to meet a variety of problems that are presented in oral or written form involving the different language and the different procedures that will be represented by the symbol '÷'. Consider the procedures for solving the following problems (see Figures 5.3a and 5.3b) and the associated discussion that may take place:

(a) 12 marbles are to be shared equally among 3 children. How many marbles will each child get?

(a) 12 marbles shared among 3 children

(b) 12 marbles are to be packaged into boxes of 3. How many boxes will be needed?

(b) 12 marbles boxed in threes

Figure 5.3

Not only are the sharing and grouping solution procedures different for each problem, but the visual images present at the end of each procedure is different. In the first problem the 'answer', 4, is the number of marbles in front of each child. In the second problem the 'answer', 4, is the number of groups of marbles when they are arranged in threes. Children will need to think through the solution procedure and be able to 'read' the result in each situation if understanding of division is to develop.

Although it is usual for children to identify division with sharing in the sense of the first illustration above, some interesting discussion may arise if this is not a common interpretation for all the group. A teacher working with 10- and 11-year-olds asked them how they would explain to a 7-year-old how to solve the problem 12 ÷ 3 using counters or cubes as they thought appropriate. Groups from the class were asked to 'demonstrate' their explanations to the rest of the class and then make posters to show their methods. Although the majority approached the problem through sharing, much discussion arose when one group used a grouping approach generating the different visual images and using alternative descriptions of the procedure. Discussing division problems as they are attempted will enable the children to verbalize their thinking, developing appropriate language under the guidance of a teacher and their peers.

Meanings of the symbol

Symbols need to be *read* and *interpreted* with words or phrases being used to convey the *meanings* of arithmetic expressions. If we take the operation of division as our example, the symbol '÷' as used in the expression '12 ÷ 3' may be read in many ways. The word 'share' will almost certainly be one that is associated with division. Although the word 'divide' will be less familiar to most young children there is a growing acceptance and use of this interpretation as children get older. So what does the word 'divide' mean and what are the procedures for division? Again the answers are complex and children's understanding will develop through negotiation of meanings with teachers and with peers as they experience a range of problems related to division. As the illustrations above indicate, the word 'share' is not a direct replacement for the word 'divide' although many division experiences will be based on sharing. The variety of language is daunting as the following discussion will reveal.

The language that children use

Recording children and teachers as they work on division tasks has shown some of the wide variation in the phrases used to read and interpret the division symbol. The following common phrases involving the word 'divide' or 'divided' are frequently used:

12 divided by 3	12 divided into 3
12 divide by 3	12 divide into 3
	12 divided into 3s

Compare first the phrases '12 divided by 3' and '12 divide by 3'. The *passive* construction 'divided by' may be replaced by the *active* construction 'divide by' to indicate a procedure that may be implemented to solve the problem. This preference for active sentence constructions is well-known and has been noted earlier in this chapter for the phrases used for multiplication. In the images children associate with such actions it may be indicated that three people are involved as 12 is 'divided by' 3 (people) or it may relate to a single person actively involved in the process of dividing.

Just as a pizza may be 'divided into' three portions, some children appear to associate division with partitioning *into* equal subsets and use this phrase in their interpretation. There is a subtle difference implicit in the phrases '12 divided into 3' and '12 divided into 3s' where the first may be identified with a sharing procedure resulting in 3 'portions' while the second suggests a grouping procedure or repeated subtraction of 3s (resulting in 4 'portions'). Another anecdote illustrates how solution procedures appropriate for some problems may present difficulties in others.

Lisa and Anna, both ten years old, were trying to solve the problem

$$6000 \div 6 = ?$$

Having consistently read the symbol '÷' as 'divided by' and successfully tackled the problems $28 \div 7 =$ and $35 \div 5 =$ using their table facts, they have agreed that the question read '6000 divided by 6' and asked 'how many sixes are there in six thousand?'. Failing to solve the problem on paper, they collect together structured apparatus of rods and blocks to represent six piles of one thousand cubes each. Their next step is to start removing groups of six to see how many sixes there are. Clearly this was a very inefficient strategy (even if there were any hope of the pair being accurate!) and the teacher intervened as follows:

T: How many cubes do you have in front of you?

L: Six thousand.

T: How many piles of cubes do you see?

L: Six.

T: And how many in each pile?

L: A thousand.

T: So what is six thousand divided by six?

L: We don't know, so we are just going to find out.

She and Anna proceed to remove sixes but abandon their effort some minutes later.

Another 10-year-old could not understand the difficulty having read the problem as '6000 divided into 6' clearly saw that the answer must be 1000.

Although the phrase '12 divided by 3' is acknowledged to be *mathematically correct*, most teachers would agree that the phrases above are all acceptable and may question the value of monitoring such apparently insignificant variations. For many children, the variations enable flexibility in approaches to solving problems but some children may become inhibited by close adherence to limited interpretations. In the examples above the problem '6000 ÷ 6' is straightforward if you imagine the total 'shared' into 6 portions of 1000 but difficult if you try to establish how many sixes can be 'found' in six thousand. On the other hand the problem '6 ÷ ½' is probably best solved by asking the question 'how many halves can be 'found' in six since the idea of 'sharing by' a half is conceptually difficult.

As well as these phrases using derivatives of the verb 'to divide' there appear to be a wealth of alternatives used by children:

shared into 3, shared into 3s, shared by 3, shared with 3
split into 3, split into 3s
how many 3s in 12, 3 into 12, 3s into 12
12 grouped in 3, 12 grouped into 3s, 12 grouped in 3

(It is worth noting that the phrase '12 shared with 3' is likely to match the image of a share and 3 friends and so 4 recipients altogether!)

The phrase 'How many threes are there in twelve?' is sometimes used to interpret the symbols 12 ÷ 3 and this appears to be an *indirect* interpretation relating to multiplication, not only because the numbers are reversed but also because it is indicating a solution strategy for the problem rather than interpreting the symbols. This interpretation may provide one of the keys to link division to multiplication as inverse operations. This interpretation may also give meaning to division problems where the divisor is fractional, e.g. 'How many halves are there in 6?' But it has been seen that this same interpretation may inhibit children's solutions as in the problem $6000 \div 6$: 'How many sixes are there in 6000?'.

It appears that teachers may 'accept' many different phrases from children while themselves using the formal interpretation 'divided by'. Recorded conversations in the classroom illustrate this point.

Salim was having difficulty with the problem $68 \div 17$ when his teacher tried to help:

T: What does it say Salim?

S: 68 shared into 17.

T: That's right, 68 divided by 17. How many 17s in 68?

S: Umm.

T: What is twice 17, Salim?

S: 34.

T: Now can you see how many 17s make 68?

The teacher's assumption here was that Salim could shift from sharing to grouping to doubling, all as possible solution procedures for division. The phrase 'divided by' was used by the teacher in relation to a particular interpretation of the phrase while the pupil used the specific phrase 'shared into'. Teachers using the mathematical terminology 'divided by' will need to help children *interpret* this phrase and will *negotiate* extended meanings as the individual appears ready to progress in understanding the complexity of the terms. This will require teachers to assess children's existing understanding and use appropriate examples and explanations, involving apparatus and pictorial representation to explore the interpretations that may be made.

Clearly the interpretation given to a particular problem will influence greatly the solution strategy selected but it appears that the words used by children may or may not indicate the procedure they have in mind. Some children adopt a single strategy as the example involving Lisa and Anna illustrates. Some employ a wide range of strategies paying little attention to the words that are used but understanding the diversity of meanings that may be associated with the division symbol. It is here that significant differences appear to exist between higher and lower achieving children. Able children appear to be able to *select* an interpretation and solution strategy to suit each individual problem while others do not progress from a particular strategy that has given them early success. Opportunities to share their thinking with others will encourage children to reflect on the methods and language they themselves use and become aware of alternative interpretations and strategies. Encouraged by teachers, the children can learn effectively by reviewing their own thinking and that of their peers.

In order to promote thinking and discussion of division problems I have found the following activity very effective. Getting the children to work in groups the teacher provides a list of the following problems and asks them to discuss which they find easy and which they find hard:

$24 \div 4 =$
$34 \div 7 =$
$6000 \div 6 =$
$6 \div 12 =$

How many 30g servings can you get from a 500g packet of cornflakes?

$68 \div 17 =$
$800 \div 50 =$
$396 \div 3 =$
$4 \div \frac{1}{2} =$

The children are not asked to find answers (though they almost inevitably do as the discussion progresses) but to rank the problems in order from the easiest to the hardest. The groups are asked to agree on the ordering having discussed the reasons why some are easy and some are harder. Listening to the discussions that follow will show teachers that the reasons children give are very varied, from the security some children find in problems relating to pencil and paper procedures (e.g. $396 \div 3 =$) to reasons based on the lack of awareness that order matters ($6 \div 12 =$) and the predictable discomfort of a word problem. From the discussions that are involved, children and their teachers can gain substantial insight into the thinking processes of others and the language and meanings of the symbols involved. Whole classes can be involved if the different groups are asked to report on their discussion and their agreed ranking of the problems. Where a teacher is able to note the thinking of individual children, there is a wealth of follow-up work to clarify misunderstandings and to provide those who show sound understanding with more challenging tasks.

Teachers may decide whether or not calculators are to be available for this activity. Where the purpose of the task is to discuss relative ease of the problems, a calculator may provide a tool for exploring suggestions and confirming individual claims and may stimulate further discussion that will expose language and thinking. The shock for some children when $6 \div 12$ does not turn out to be 2 must be reconciled with the evident infallibility of a calculator. The answer to the word problem, 'How many 30g servings can you get from a 500g packet of cornflakes?' as '16.666666' will need to be interpreted in the context of the question that is asked. Many other considerations are involved when the calculator is used as an aid to thinking.

Calculators and calculating aids

Calculators are frowned upon in some circles for preventing children from thinking and from undertaking their own calculations. While it is true that a calculator gives an immediate correct response to problems, it is necessary to input the problem using the appropriate symbols and to interpret the display after a calculation. Word problems that relate to real situations rarely involve the mathematical terminology that relates to the symbols on the calculator. The cornflakes problem above makes no mention of division and the order of the numbers in the question is the reverse of the order to be keyed in for calculation. Problems like '$4 \div \frac{1}{2} =$ ' cannot be directly keyed in to most calculators as fractions are usually not recognized and children will need to consider ways to interpret this problem just as they will need to interpret the solution to many others like '$34 \div 7 =$ ' and '$6 \div 12 =$ '.

The calculator can provide each child with an important personal tool that acts under instruction and provides rapid non-threatening feedback. Using calculators enables children to use symbols and experience patterns of number behaviour associated with the four operations of arithmetic. Take, for example, the pattern of multiplying by ten. It is easy to predict that 'multiplying by ten results in adding a nought on the end' until this conjecture is tested on such numbers as 0.2 or 0.05. With the aid of a calculator, children can investigate such results, they can predict and conjecture and formulate their thinking in written form or by expressing their thoughts to others.

Calculators can not only take the labour out of calculation, they can also release time in school to allow children to come to terms with other extremely important aspects of calculation which are often not treated as thoroughly as is needed. These aspects include: what each operation means, which particular operation to use in particular situations and how to apply the answer back to the problem situation.

Calculators provide an important learning aid that will supplement but should not replace pencil and paper efforts and other aids like structured apparatus. Although it is time-consuming, giving children objects to help them formulate their thinking and produce representations of abstract problems will provide tactile and visual experiences that make a lasting impression. Some children find it a lot easier to explain their thinking if they have equipment available to touch and move so that they can *describe* their actions rather than try to formulate abstract thoughts. These objects also provide images that make it easier for children to follow the thinking of others and to recall situations that they have experienced before.

The way forward

Language has become an important consideration for the mathematics teacher as the constructivist paradigm for learning is widely acknowledged to be the effective framework for learning. The silent mathematics classroom with every child working independently on abstract calculations has limitations in its value for effective learning, and environments that encourage communication will provide a more appropriate preparation for a role in society today. For the interested reader, Pimm (1987) takes this discussion further in his book, *Speaking Mathematically: Communication in Mathematics Classrooms*.

It is the nature of mathematics that concise communication is achieved through the use of symbols and formalized 'expressions' to convey information and to pose questions. However, the route to understanding such mathematics is by successively broadening children's experiences of the language and meanings associated with formal mathematical expressions. The symbols of arithmetic (e.g. $+$, $-$, $\times$, $\div$, $=$) enable conciseness in communication by providing a 'shorthand' for written work and later provide a form of representation that enables an algorithmic (pencil and paper calculation) approach to the solution of problems. Children must come to know that each symbol may be interpreted using a variety of language that relate to different solution procedures for problems. Taking division again as the example, it may be seen that the different phrases that are available to interpret the symbol '÷' will indicate some of the different methods of solution that are possible:

12 ÷ 3 How many threes in twelve
3000 ÷ 3 3000 shared *into* 3
6 ÷ ½ How many halves in 6
6 ÷ 12 6 shared *by* 12

A child who has a single-solution strategy will find problems that are not easily accessible like 68 ÷ 17 =   or 31 ÷ 16 =   , neither of which respond easily to sharing procedures.

So it is important for children to hear and to use a diversity of language for each of the arithmetic symbols, and for teachers to monitor their progress in understanding, negotiating new meanings for symbols in different contexts. The way forward will be facilitated where teachers are able to listen and learn from their pupils as the pupils learn from them. It is just as important that children become proficient with the language of arithmetic as the calculation procedures that are involved if they are to make sense of numbers. Just as a language is learned as an interconnection of words and phrases rather than isolated expressions (however useful these may be in specific circumstances), so the relationships that exist among numbers have interdependence that must be considered and discussed if real understanding is to develop.

REFERENCES

Anghileri, J. (1990) 'Language of multiplication' in Durkin, K. and Shire, B. *Language and Mathematics Education.* Milton Keynes: Open University Press.

Carpenter, T., Moser, J. and Romberg, T. (eds) (1982) *Addition and Subtraction: a Cognitive Perspective.* New Jersey: Laurence Erlbaum.

DES and Welsh Office (1989) *Mathematics in the National Curriculum – Non-Statutory Guidance.* London: HMSO.

NCTM (National Council of Teachers of Mathematics) (1989) *USA Curriculum and Evaluation Standards for School Mathematics.* Virginia: NCTM.

Pimm, D. (1987) *Speaking Mathematically: Communication in Mathematics Classrooms.* London: Routledge and Kegan Paul.

Shuard, H. and Rothery, A. (1984) *Children Reading Mathematics.* London: John Murray.

Von Glaserfeld, E. (1990) 'Environment and communication' in Steffe, L. and Wood, T. (eds) *Transforming Children's Mathematics Education: International Perspectives.* Hillsdale, NJ: Laurence Erlbaum.

CHAPTER 6

CAN Calculators Make a Difference?

LAURIE ROUSHAM

Ask a primary teacher to describe an art lesson and you get a wide variety of responses. Several different types of session seem to take place, and it is possible to classify most of them under a few main headings. Sometimes a skill or technique is being taught, and progressing towards mastery of this skill is clearly the purpose of the lesson. At other times, things are very free and the expectation is that the children will produce something – they will 'do some art'. In some of these 'creative' sessions the teacher may constrain the situation by specifying the medium or the materials to be used, but children have a large measure of choice and creative control and the main purpose is to allow them to experiment and to use what they already know. Children's experience of art is thus likely to take many different forms, varying from complete freedom to 30 almost identical artefacts pinned up on the wall. Some teachers work mainly in one style, some in another, but the main impression is one of variety.

Ask about mathematics, however, and you tend to get overwhelmingly the equivalent of the *first* kind of art session described above: the learning and practice of skills and techniques in isolation. If we taught art that way exclusively, I think children's attitudes to art might deteriorate sharply. How can we provide for children a greater variety of sessions in maths?

I have been looking at some of the mathematical activities that went on at Stutton Primary school near Ipswich, in Suffolk where I worked during the CAN (Calculator-Aware Number) Curriculum Project. I find I can classify many of them in a similar way to the art activities described earlier. Some were structured or constrained to some extent by the teacher, but many offered children a real chance to be creative with the mathematics they already knew. Once the children became used to this style of activity they often managed to be remarkably creative and original within the supposedly 'structured' situations too. If a mixture of structured and creative styles provides a better atmosphere and environment for the learning of art than either one in isolation, why not mathematics too? Of course, I want children to learn new techniques and skills in maths, just as I do in art: equally, I want them sometimes to have freedom to put these into practice in a more creative activity.

Background to CAN

The Calculator-Aware Number (CAN) Project set out to devise a curriculum in the area of number which would take account of the power of the calculator as a teaching tool. Its aims would lie in ... developing the primary mathematics curriculum for children who will live out their adult lives in the twenty-first century.' (Shuard, 1986, p. 1)

CAN ran from 1986 to 1989 and its work was then continued in the CAN Continuation Project. CAN was initiated by Hilary Shuard and directed by her from Homerton College, Cambridge until her death in 1993. The impact of this project has been recognized around the world. In the project schools, every child was provided with a calculator and allowed free choice as and when to use it. No algorithms, i.e. particular set methods for the four rules of number, were to be taught. Instead, children would be encouraged to devise, and to share, their own ways of solving addition, subtraction, multiplication and division problems, with a strong emphasis on mental methods of calculation. The results of CAN are well reported elsewhere, both by the project team (Shuard *et al.*, 1991) and by the national evaluator whose annual Reports for the National Curriculum Council have been published in one volume (Duffin, 1994). In this chapter I am concerned to think about some of the activities which sprang from the classrooms involved in the project; what kinds of things teachers did when there was no published scheme in use and they did not have to spend a lot of time showing, or trying to show, children 'how to do' subtraction, multiplication and so on.

At the beginning of the project some teachers wondered what there would be left to teach if we were not going to be teaching algorithms – after all, that's what primary schools spend most of their 'number time' doing. I remember someone asking Hilary this question at an early meeting. Closing her eyes and tilting her head back, she gave her broadest grin and said: 'All that's left will be ... mathematics!' She was right, and teachers found a lot to do which proved to be more worthwhile than our previous practice. But CAN did not mean simply handing out calculators, then standing back to see what happens, rather like you do when you light a firework. It was much more carefully structured. Despite early worries about what we would teach, we found ourselves far more closely and meaningfully involved with our children and their mathematics than ever before. Because much of what used to dominate maths time had been shorn away, we did have to find some new things for children to do. Many of these were devised collaboratively, at the regular teacher meetings which were such a powerful and supportive feature of CAN. Often they were adaptations of things we had done before. Sometimes they were structured activities set up by the teachers in order to promote or investigate a particular area of mathematics, but many corresponded better to the freer, more creative sessions described by teachers when talking about art.

After a year or so in CAN, children began to ask 'Can I do some maths?' as they would ask to do a painting. Subject to teacher consent, they could then go off and devise mathematical activities for them-selves. This was not something the children had felt able (or inclined) to do before, though for most of them it took several terms before they felt confident enough to invent problems for themselves or for a friend. These would probably be based on the kinds of things they had been doing in lessons, but it was exciting to see them wanting to do maths for the pleasure of exploring numbers. At Stutton we had a few parents who jokingly complained that their children's enthusiasm for maths was causing problems. 'We haven't read her reading book' said one 'because all she wants to do is maths.' Another wrote of 'Maths at the breakfast table ... maths in the bath even!'

Making possible this kind of creative freedom within a mathemat-ical context not only extended the options available to teachers but greatly increased the variety of mathematical situations encountered by the children. At Stutton, it certainly also increased their enjoyment and changed attitudes to the subject.

In the rest of this chapter I will give examples of what I mean by 'structured' and 'creative' activities and try to indicate some of the questions that arise when we consider the way in which calculator use can affect children's thinking about number.

Structured activity with calculators

A common *structured* activity which I used was to ask the children each to write down twelve or so numbers in a list, encouraging diversity. 'I don't mind what you put down – your age, your door number. My door number's 46, put that down … put down a big number, a small number, your favourite number … remember, the person next to you will be starting with a different list, so don't turn to her and be surprised if she has different answers to you – you are probably both right!' Once the children had compiled their lists, I might say, 'Right, this table, I want you to multiply all your numbers by 10; this table, please add 10 to all yours; this table add zero to them all; you lot multiply by 1 …' etc. The children would not need telling that they could use their calculators for this. Some would opt to do it mentally, but most would run their list through the machine. Each table's task was to figure out what was happening, look for any patterns they might find and, *when everyone in that group was all agreed*, explain to me what was going on. It did not take very many of the numbers to be processed before somebody on each table was coming up with a hypothesis, usually along the lines of 'I don't need the calculator to do this, look …' and once the whole table was convinced about how to add 10, multiply by 10, add zero or whatever it was I wanted them to explore that day, they could call me over and try to convince me. Using this type of activity frequently made sure each group had experience of seeing what happens in the case of multiplying by 1, 0, 5, 10, adding 10 and multiples of 10 and so on.

This kind of pattern spotting is encouraged in mathematics National Curricula and National Guidelines, but allowing the use of the calculator makes it much more powerful. It means that children can see the effect of an operation on more numbers than they could ever do before, so they have much more data. Not only this, but they are literally 'seeing' it come up on the calculator's display screen. The entire number system is built into a calculator, place value particularly, and by using it a lot, much incidental information about how numbers behave and are changed by the various operations is absorbed in a way that is qualitatively different from working from a printed page.

Sometimes a group would go on and on, testing many more numbers than the dozen or so I had asked them to generate at the beginning, before being convinced. Had I required them to calculate each example themselves, calculation would have become the end rather than the means. Some would have made mistakes. Others started chatting. Either way their attention would not be focused on what was happening to their original list of numbers. Once the children knew that the means of calculation were under their control, a fierce interest in numbers, patterns and how they behaved began to develop.

Many people have expressed anxiety that children will become dependent upon the calculator as a result of being allowed to use them before they know all about calculations. The CAN experience demonstrated that this need not be the case. Consider the following extract from a tape recording of a different 'structured' activity. I had set some 'missing number' problems such as $25 + ? = 53$, and the three children (aged 6 and 7) on this particular table had finished them all correctly, so I went over to talk to them.

LR: Well done. How did you do this one? [$23 + ? = 50$]

Matt: I tried 33 and it came to 56 so I took away 7 and I put 33–7 and it made 26.

LR: Why d'you take away 7?

Robert: [Addressing Matt] It's 6 too many.

Chris: [Interrupting] I did it in my head, I tried 39 and it made 62, so I said to myself, take away 9, that was wrong [doing it on calculator as he speaks] ... 53, so ... that's when I decided not to use the calculator.

LR: Can you show me how you did it?

Chris: No.

LR: O.K, what about $14 + ? = 25$? Try that.

Chris: [Using calculator] Sixteen, no, it's too many.

Robert: [Mentally] Eleven.

Chris: I'll try 13, no it's too many ...

LR: Try 10. [Because I knew that they had recently done the activity described above, i.e. adding 10 to a list of numbers]

Chris: [Mentally] No, that would only give you 24 ...

Robert: [Getting impatient] Eleven!

Chris: Oh, yes, it is 11; 10, and 1 more!

For me, Chris' last remark was the payoff. I was pleased that he and Matt had carried on wanting to solve my fresh problem, ignoring the correct answer given to them by Robert quite early on. Chris seems able to remember his earlier work on adding a ten, perhaps suddenly seeing the usefulness of it in this calculation. Whether or not this extract shows the transfer of a previously acquired piece of know-ledge, gained from the earlier structured activity, is open to question. What I think it does provide is a counter-example to the initial fears of some people both inside and outside the project that children would become dependent upon the machines and be helpless without them.

The feedback loop

A significant feature of many calculator activities is that they encourage what might be called a 'feedback loop'. It rests on the fact that the machine gives information in response to 'questions', provided you know how to question it. What number must you add to 14 in order to get to 25: is it 16, perhaps? Well, one way to find out is to 'ask' the calculator. Not only does the machine silently 'answer' this question in the negative, it gives a fresh and unasked-for piece of information via its display: '30'. Fourteen and 16 comes to 30, not 50. Check it – yes there it is again. Hmm. The machine silently offers the information that $14 + 16 = 30$ and the initiative is back with the child, who must think what to make of this, perhaps assimilating it with a piece of existing knowledge, like the fact that $4 + 6 = 10$. This can help to key in a new 'question'. CAN children became adept at using the feedback loop, partly because many of the activities (including the 23 + ? activity described above) were intended to get them into using it. They learned to enter a number which they thought would be roughly right, then proceed on a trial-and-improve basis to home in on the exact answer. This is what Chris is doing in lines 13 and 15 of the transcript when he keys in 16 and, seeing 30 on his display, says 'no, it's too many'.

Notice, however, that what I mean by the feedback loop is something more than, and clearly distinct from, the trial-and-improve method. It is fairly easy to show children how to use trial-and-improve in the above situation, but they may or may not utilize the incidental information which the calculator offers them during the process. One characteristic of 'loop' information is that it is unsolicited, and may be ignored if you are in a hurry, if you are only interested in the final result, or if you cannot at the moment fit it into what you already know. The machine just works in the way that it does. Children work in very individual ways and have different reactions and internal explanations for what is being displayed in the course of a calculation. Most adults never use a calculator enough to tune in to the feedback loop and, in simple tasks at least, they already know more than the machine is 'telling' them. They ignore the process of interplay between fingers and display to concentrate on the end result. Children work slower and are more interested in transient displays during the course of a long calculation. They soon learn, for example that in the course of adding a series of numbers, the calculator keeps a running total as you go along.

Try it for yourself: 269 + 147 + 19.4 + 8. Yes, the 'answer' is 443.4, but the machine also tells you that 269 +147 is 416, as soon as you press the plus key for the second time. When you press it a third time, before entering the eight, another interim total (435.4) is displayed. I have watched children sit and think about what is displayed, sometimes doing a mental check, sometimes seeing for the first time how it looks when you add in a decimal, sometimes reversing an operation to get back to whole numbers. The learning potential of all this is much greater if they are in the course of a long calculation involving all four operations, especially one which includes a decimal number or two. Many adults who learned to calculate with pencil and paper could benefit from doing some of this, watching the display, talking about what was happening, and why. Children certainly can, but they need sufficient confidence and familiarity with the machines over time, if calculator activities are to be more than a meaningless novelty.

Creative activity with calculators

I have given two examples of activities where a considerable amount of structure is provided by the teacher. An example of a more 'creative' activity would be that called 'making numbers' in Suffolk but which will be familiar to many teachers under a variety of names. It is also a good example of how teachers took over or adapted existing activities and then found the fact that children were doing them with calculators led both parties into all sorts of new territory. Essentially it consists of saying to the class something like: 'The answer is 36; what is the question?' so that they are challenged to 'make' 36, but in as many different possible ways as they can.

I talked to Daniel, a 7-year-old experienced calculator user who was carrying out this activity. In response to my question 'Do you mind telling me about what you are doing?' he replied: 'I'm making 8.'

He had filled almost three pages of his maths book with long strings of calculations, all of which ended firmly ' = 8' and included all four operations and numbers like −0.5 as well as long decimal displays and six-figure whole numbers. As I watched him dividing by 600 I asked:

LR: When you're trying out all these things, don't you ever think you'll never get back to eight?

Daniel: I can always get back to eight. I can get back to eight any time I want to. See, this [the calculator] is like a video recorder.

This stumped me, wondering if he meant he kept information in the memory or something but, seeing my puzzled look, he went on:

Daniel: You see THIS key [add button] is like, PLAY. Now this key [multiplication sign] is like fast-forward. The take away key is rewind . . . and this one [division sign] is fast rewind. So I just use them to make the numbers go up and down and, when I feel like it . . . when I've had enough . . . I make it come to eight.

There is a very strong sense of imagery here. Daniel also spoke of 'zooming up and down' as he called it, in both positive and negative directions, but his own casual account perhaps does him less than justice. In a sense you could say he is 'just' trying out the effect of different operations and exotic numbers, but a look at his recording showed, for example, that he knew how to get rid of the decimal fractions using subtraction, so as to return to whole numbers for the eight. When he wanted to home in on his chosen number, the choices of numbers and operations were good ones to get him there fast. His calculator did the number crunching and displayed the result of each operation as he went along, thus providing possibly interesting new information by way of the feedback loop but it was Daniel who decided, after some thought each time, just what to key in next. He looked constantly from the book where he was recording each operation and number, to the display, which told him the result of what he had done and showed the new running total so that, if it was in the tens of thousands for example, he might choose something which he knew would sharply reduce it – like the division by 600 mentioned earlier.

Daniel had chosen to do this activity and was obviously revelling in the element of freedom to experiment which it allowed him. To me, his video analogy seems to suggest the idea of a number line, but this may be to impose something which is not there. It is possible, for example, that it comes more simply and straightforwardly from watching the numbers of the videotape counter reel round, like a very fast mileometer, as you fast-forward or rewind the tape. What do children make of calculators and other digital displays, experiences unavailable to them a few years ago? How do they integrate them into their existing knowledge and thinking about number, and how is it shaped by them?

Availability versus access

CAN was a fairly localized project, beginning in just 20 schools, though there are now over 15,000 children working in a CAN style in England and Wales. Since CAN, the National Curriculum for England and Wales has given more widespread sanction to the use of calculators through the Statutory Orders (DES 1989a, 1991, DFE 1994) and the associated Non-Statutory Guidance, as well as their being advocated by the School's Inspectorate, HMI (DES 1989b). Support for calculators is clearly expressed in *Scottish Guidelines – Mathematics 5–14* and in the USA Standards for School Mathematics:

> Calculators must be accepted at the K-4 level (and 5–16) as valuable tools for learning mathematics ... The thoughtful use of calculators can increase the quality of the curriculum as well as the quality of children's learning (p. 19) ... These devices free students from tedious computation and allow them to concentrate on problem solving and other important content (p. 87) (NCTM, 1989)

Despite official encouragement and widespread support from mathematics educationalists (see NCTM, 1992), reports indicate that they are not being used to any great extent in many classrooms. Where they are used, it is often for disappointingly limited purposes such as checking work already done, failing to capitalize on the power of the machine as a cognitive learning tool which individuals can use to explore mathematics for themselves in exciting, and hitherto inaccessible, ways.

This position in the UK, outlined in official reports (DES 1989b, OFSTED 1993) is supported by a recent survey conducted by Warren and Ling in 25 schools in Hertfordshire. Warren and Ling (1994) found that 'the adoption of the use of calculators has not been as widespread as might have been expected'. Hertfordshire publishes materials for teachers to use, including an excellent booklet called *The Calculator Collection* (Parr, 1990). This contains a good discussion of the ways in which calculators have been found to be helpful as well as a number of photocopiable activities of the more powerful kind. Given that Warren and Ling's work was carried out in an area where such encouragement has been available, it would be surprising if the picture in other Education Authorities was very different, particularly given the continuing decline in advisory support for teachers at classroom level in the UK, and the overloading of primary teachers in England and Wales by initiatives, directives and changes following the introduction of the National Curriculum in 1989.

The situation in the USA appears to be no more promising and 'the pace of calculator-induced change in school curricula has been very slow' (NCTM, 1992). This is despite the fact that 'the preponderance of research evidence supports the fact that calculator use for instruction and testing enhances learning and performance of arithmetic concepts and skills, problem solving and attitudes of students' (Hembree and Dessart, 1992)

In addition, the situation is more complex than the simple issue of the existence of calculators in schools. I have myself surveyed teachers on a smaller scale, asking 'Are calculators available to your pupils?' The answer is almost always 'yes'. Teachers in England and Wales have got the message that calculators are in some way a 'good thing' and most say that calculators are available in their classes. If however, the *children* in those classes are asked whether calculators are available to them when they need one, a very different picture emerges, one which could be roughly summarized as 'Calculators? What calculators?' There is a difference between 'availability' and 'access'. Teachers tend to interpret my question as meaning 'Are calculators available to you?' despite the inclusion of the wording 'to your pupils'. Thus, availability is generally taken to refer to the situation from the teacher's perspective, as in:

We have them available for when we wish to use them
They are available, but I don't use them myself
I think it is important to have calculators available because they will
have to be familiar with them when they leave school.

I will use 'access', as distinct from 'availability', to denote the degree to which *pupils* are allowed use of a calculator in their mathematical learning.

Why are teachers not giving real access to children? One possible reason may lie in anecdotal evidence from teachers who were involved in the CAN project. This frequently mentions the degree to which calculator access gave children a large measure of control over their own learning. To some teachers this was a stimulus and a challenge, but nevertheless it was also a cause of some anxiety. For a few, it was extremely threatening. If this was true within a large, nationally funded project which went out of its way to support the teachers involved, perhaps it is not surprising that even in 1994, some teachers appear to prefer to keep control of such powerful little machines. Added to this are the understandable anxieties about possible harmful effects and worries about what parents or the media will make of it. Teachers in CAN schools shared such feelings in the early stages, but all the evidence from the project confirms the role of the calculator as a powerful, individual learning tool and an investigational device in schools rather than as a crutch for those who are already unsure or failing in mathematics.

We should also be aware that it is difficult to enter the child's perceptions and understanding of ideas such as 'access' as used here. One teacher, an enthusiastic user of calculators in her teaching, has a telling story. She regularly stressed to her class that they could use them whenever they felt they would be helpful and often put a number of machines out on a central table before commencing an activity, together with cubes and other possibly useful apparatus. Later, carrying out a survey of her children's perceptions as part of a 20-day course in mathematics, she was taken aback to discover that because she put them out sometimes (but not always) the children had assumed that if they were not put out, then they were not to be used.

Crossing the threshold

What is disappointing is not simply that the incidence of calculator use is so low. In the period since 1989 many teachers simply have not had the time to experiment or incorporate this particular innovation into their teaching. That may be expected to change, if slowly, over time. It is rather that children need real access over some considerable time to become sufficiently familiar and confident with them to cross that 'threshold' of familiarity which allows them to use the calculator's power for the kind of higher order exploration of tasks which I noticed children doing during the CAN project. It is important that we do not underestimate this.

I can still observe sophisticated usage happening in post-CAN schools where the children have become used to having real access to calculators, but in situations where calculators are used occasionally and infrequently, it seems that it is very difficult to provide sufficient access for children to cross that threshold. The notion of a threshold is one which is commonly found in studies of the effects of other forms of technology, such as the ImpacT Report from King's College, London (Watson, 1993). This looked at information technology across the curriculum, analysing its effects upon a range of subject areas at both primary and secondary levels.

To illustrate both sides of the calculator threshold more clearly, I will present two examples. One is from a school which uses calculators 'fairly frequently'; the other from a school where the children take them for granted as they do rulers or multilink. In both schools I worked with groups of 8- and 9-year-old children who were judged by their teachers to be of middle ability in mathematics. None were perceived as high-flyers, but nor did any have special difficulties. I gave them an activity adapted from one used by the Assessment of Performance Unit (Foxman, 1988) to assess group problem solving.

The children are led to discover a rule, then use it to generate a chain of numbers. The rule is: If it's odd, add 3; if it's even, halve it, and keep on applying this rule to the answers you get. They can start with any (whole) number they like, e.g. $46 > 23 > 26 > 13 > 16$, etc. In every case a chain is formed which eventually goes into one of two loops; either $6 > 3 > 6 > 3$; or $4 > 2 > 1 > 4 > 2 > 1$. Their task would be to generate chains, spot the loops, then investigate which numbers go into which loops. (All multiples of 3 eventually go $6 > 3$;

children usually say 'It's the 3 times table'. All other numbers go into the $4 > 2 > 1$ loop.)

The following extract comes from the school where the children do almost all their mathematics without calculators. The children are having problems halving some of their bigger two-digit numbers.

LR: We're talking about, this same halving problem that nearly everybody in the group is ... has had this problem at some point.

Ellie: Thirty-five?

LR: Thirty-five. Is that half of 32?

Ellie: No- I mean- I mean 25, hang on ... no ...

LR: Twenty-five, might that be half ... so ... um ... half of 32 we want.

Martin: Half of 32? Ea-sy! [begins to hum]

Ellie: Got 31, we've already done 31, so ... 32 that must be um.

LR: A half, we want a half.

Susie: Half 30 first.

Shirelle: I've got 36 ...

LR: What's the, er ...

Susie: – and then that could be ... and then you could add two on to it.

LR: What's the er, I mean, you lot are pretty good at halving numbers up to 20, it seems to me. If I say, six, you know what ...

Ellie: I've got it! ... well, 32, – half of that is 16.

LR: Why is, why is it 16?

Ellie: I don't know. [laughs]

LR: Well how did you get it?

Ellie: I done it with the calculator.

LR: Now, your calculator's still saying 32. How did you make it tell you that it was 16?

Ellie: Well, what I do is, sort of think like a number like, I said 18 which is, um, 18 add 18 equals ... and that was 36. And so it must be a lower number than that. And I've just, I've just, um, I got, I just chose 16, add 16 equals, 32. That's how I got it.

LR: That's really brilliant Ellie! Does everyone understand Ellie's method? She tries any old number, well, one she thinks is roughly right – and if it's too big she tries a smaller one, and if it's too small . . .

All: She tries a bigger one!

This group went on to try to use Ellie's method, but got into all sorts of trouble. She understood what she was doing, but was not able to communicate it to the others. These children have neither the mental ability to halve the numbers nor the calculator facility to generate the data for the loops. Ellie discovers and describes the feedback loop (lines 23–27) and uses it to devise a trial-and-improve method for halving, but we ran out of time and the loops investigation had to be abandoned. In my experience, responses such as these are not uncommon. Children who have not crossed the familiarity threshold with regard to calculator use and who cannot halve numbers like 72 mentally, frequently do not realize that this is something a calculator can do, saying such things as 'But it hasn't got a halving button' if reminded that they have calculators available.

Changing now to the group which has taken access to calculators for granted since they entered school, contrast the degree of familiarity, not just with the calculator's functions, powers and possibilities, but the intuitive sureness about numbers and how they work (and the higher order calculator use) in the following extract. The children are of the same age (8- to 9-years-old) and similar ability according to their teachers' perceptions. The group was working on the same 'loops' investigation. Halving was not a problem for them as they knew that they could divide by two on the calculator. Each of the six children had tried out several starting numbers and had generated a page or two of chains, which eventually went into one or other of the loops. I asked them to tell me which numbers went into which loops and they had been working on this individually for some minutes, when Joanne came up with a hypothesis:

Joanne: I think they're all three times table numbers.

Jamell: They are!
[The other children begin checking Joanne's and Jamell's statements]
Katie: They're not. I thought that, but they're not.

[This throws everybody, including me! Katie is asked how she knows]

Katie: Well, 255 goes 4 > 2 > 1.

[Silence for a moment and then, with groans, the group accepts that this disproves Joanne's case. I am interested in why Katie tried 255]

LR: How d'you know 255 was in the three times table?

Katie: Well, I did this, you know ... [keys in 3 + + on my calculator and presses the equals key repeatedly] ... and 255 is eighty-five threes.
[Note also the absence of adult intervention to stimulate discussion]

Had Katie's data been right, she would have disproved Joanne's (correct) hypothesis by her counter-example. In fact, she had made a slip in working out the chain for 255. Working fast, she had written:

$$255 > 258 > 129 > 132 > 66 > 33 > 36 > 18 > 9 > 12 > 4 > 2 > 1$$

If she had divided by two on an odd number, the calculator would have alerted her by displaying a decimal. If she had mistakenly added three to one of the even numbers, she would have generated a new number but it would still have been within the table of threes. In fact, she has done neither of these – she has jumped from twelve to four, when she should have halved and gone into the 6 > 3 loop which would have supported Joanne's conjecture. In fact it was Joanne who discovered the mistake, working through the chain for 255 herself because she could hardly believe that Katie was right. When this was pointed out to her, Katie said she could not imagine why she had made such a silly mistake. Perhaps she had the number three in her mind when she got to twelve, and wrote down a four by a kind of number bond association, because three fours make twelve. At any rate, the group were very pleased to have resolved the mystery.

I was impressed by the confident way in which the whole group appeared to understand the variety of different machines they were using and exploited their capabilities. These children possessed a shared culture and knowledge that was not available to the earlier group, knowing exactly, for example, what Katie had been up to when she set up the constant to generate the table of threes. (Almost all calculators have a constant facility but Katie had been using a Texas Instruments Galaxy-9x, which performs the additional service of displaying the number of times the constant has been used, so that she could see an 85 to the left of her display and 255 on the right.)

I looked at her recording and she had been trying multiples of three chosen at random from this process. All of them had gone $6 > 3 > 6$ until she made her mistake on 255! It was not only the technicalities of the machine that they understood, however. They demonstrated an understanding of numbers, decimal place value and the effect of number operations that allowed them to concentrate on the key aspects of the investigation. I did not have to tell them that Katie's assertion was important: they knew that it was crucial and all of them began checking the chain for 255. They expect maths to make sense, and being told 255 had gone into the $4 > 2 > 1$ loop meant they had a mystery on their hands, just when they were all beginning to think that Joanne was right. Joanne's pleasure and relief when she found Katie's error was shared by everyone, including Katie: it was just a mistake, not the disaster it had seemed at first.

Have Joanne, Katie and the others been harmed by free access to calculators? I think not. Does it make a difference if we give calculators out to children in maths lessons? Well, no and yes. No, it will not make much difference if we only do it occasionally. But then, if we treated pencils as we do calculators, keeping them in boxes in cupboards, allowed out only with teacher permission, most children would never learn to write. Occasional use does not get children to that threshold of confidence and familiarity which allows them to do any more than they can *already* do without it. The thinking required to carry out calculations successfully is not built in to the machine. This is the calculator paradox: designed to do calculations for us, it is actually not much use to those whose mathematical education has already failed them – they are nowhere near the threshold and just don't know what to do with the machine. The 16- and 17-year-olds in shops and supermarkets who are helpless if their tills break down do not represent, despite what is often claimed, a 'calculator generation'. They are unlikely ever to have seen a calculator at primary level. Conventional maths teaching may be responsible for their unhappy state; the calculator certainly is not. Calculators (unfortunately) are not a lifejacket which can be thrown at those who have already failed at maths. I wonder how many adults, teachers included, are really across that calculator threshold?

However, there *is* a calculator generation. Daniel, Katie, Jamell and Joanne are part of it: and the oldest CAN children are currently 15 years old. To get to where Joanne and her friends are takes time. Within CAN, I remember that a couple of terms of calculator use went by before we began to notice the first stirrings of the confidence and creativity which we saw later, and which I have tried to give a flavour of here. If, however, we could get more children to cross the threshold, then yes, I believe calculators could make a revolutionary change possible: children might begin to *do* maths, instead of practising a bunch of skills just in case they ever might need to do maths in their future lives.

And all of them, from the most able to the very weakest, would also benefit from having a clearer idea of what calculators can – and can't – do. Because, if they ever *do* need to do any maths, once they escape from school, you know what they'll be using to do it, don't you?

REFERENCES

DES (1989a, 1991) and DFE (1994) *Mathematics in the National Curriculum* together with associated Non-Statutory Guidance. London: HMSO.

DES (1989b) *Aspects of Primary Education: The Teaching and Learning of Mathematics*. London: HMSO.

Duffin, J. (1994) *Calculators in the Classroom*. Reports of the National Evaluator of the CAN component of the PrIME project, 1986–89 and of the CAN Continuation Project, 1990–92. Hull: University of Hull Numeracy Centre.

Foxman, D. and Joffe, L. (1988) *Assessing Problem Solving in Small Groups: Evaluation and Assessment in Mathematics Education*, Science and Technology Education Document series no. 32. UNESCO: Division of Science Technical and Environmental Education.

Hembree, R. and Dessart, D. (1992) 'Research on calculators in mathematics education' in *NCTM Yearbook, 1992 Calculators in Mathematics Education*. Virginia: NCTM.

NCTM (1992) *NCTM Yearbook 1992 – Calculators in Mathematics Education*. Virginia: NCTM.

OFSTED (1993) *The Teaching and Learning of Number in Primary Schools*. London: HMSO.

Parr, A. (1990) *The Calculator Collection*. Hertfordshire County Council Education Department.

Rowland, T. (1994) *CAN in Suffolk: The First Six Months of a Calculator-Aware Number Curriculum* (second edition with additional material). Cambridge: Homerton College.

Shuard, H. (1986) *Primary Mathematics for Today and Tomorrow*. London: Longmans for the Schools Curriculum Development Council.

Shuard, H., Walsh, A., Goodwin, J. and Worcester, V. (1991) *Calculators, Children and Mathematics*. London: Simon and Schuster for the National Curriculum Council.

Warren, V. and Ling, J. G. (1994) 'Calculators in the primary school since the introduction of the National Curriculum'. *Mathematics Education Review*. 4, 30–40.

Watson, D. (ed.) (1993) *The ImpacT Report – An evaluation of the impact of Information Technology on children's achievements in primary and secondary schools*. London: the Department for Education and King's College London, Centre for Educational Studies.

CHAPTER 7

What is your Favourite Colour?

LIBBY JARED AND ANNE THWAITES

'What's your favourite colour?' How often have you been asked this question by a group of children diligently completing a questionnaire? Does the answer have any effect on you or on them? Is it really a worthwhile question to ask or could children be asking alternative questions which might give them some answers and insights that have real relevance? Do children understand the purpose of questionnaires and are they developing mathematical skills in handling data appropriate for the society in which they will be living?

One of the most dramatic changes in the classroom in recent years has been the introduction of computer software to enhance teaching and provide a stimulating environment for learning, particularly in mathematics (Mann and Tall, 1992). There have been changes in curriculum content to reflect the uses of technology in society and this is well-illustrated by the introduction of databases into the classroom to assist in the collection and analysis of information and the display of such data in a variety of formats. Database packages are available to store and sort data, to provide information relating to a variety of topics from dinosaurs to the local environment and to produce tables, graphs, charts and other diagrams of high quality at a keyboard command. Handling data has become one of the focuses for mathematics teaching:

> 'Collecting, organising, describing, and interpreting data, as well as making decisions and predictions on the basis of that information, are skills that are increasingly important in a society based on technology and communication. (NCTM, 1989, p. 54)

This chapter will examine young children's thinking when collecting and presenting data and will look at a range of activities which develop the skills and understanding needed to manage handling of data successfully. We attempt to show the development from a practical activity or visual image, through the language of characterization (where children's thinking is revealed) to an abstract representation in a database or graphical image (where children's thinking and understanding are shown in the form and interpretation of the database and imagery).

The relationship of a two-way movement between object and representation is an important one. Initially it is likely that a child will work from the concrete to the abstract. Here the starting point for a child is the object. By looking closely at the objects, it is possible through sorting to define the characteristics of the objects. This characterization then leads to the construction and interpretation of data representations (be it database or graphical). At a later developmental stage we also expect the return process, for the child to work (back) from the abstract to the concrete. Here the start is the data representation where, either through the analysis of graphs or interrogation of databases, interpretations of the characteristics can be made which in turn lead to defining the objects and relationships that exist among them. Both these processes may be observed and supported by the teacher; children's thinking is developing through active involvement, not only in activities and tasks set, but also through discussion and questioning.

Much of the work described in this chapter results from the authors' involvement in in-service courses, introducing data handling to practising primary school teachers.

Sorting and graphical representation

There are many ideas in mathematics which originate in sorting activities. Hilary Shuard (1994) provides a comprehensive discussion of the ways sets and sorting lead to fundamental concepts such as number, measuring and appreciation of shape and space. Such ideas may also be developed to include work with databases, where the understanding of the characteristics of an object and the language of searching are of particular importance.

If young children are given a collection of different objects, for example, a button box, the crockery in the home corner, a basket of fruit and vegetables, many of them will spend lots of time sorting the objects out into different sets. This leads us to believe that children have a natural desire to sort which presents an ideal beginning to data handling. It is in the process of deciding how objects are related and where a particular object might belong, that an understanding of the characteristics or *attributes* which the object possesses becomes clearer. This is the important first step in offering the opportunity for characterization to take place. Children's conversation can often offer the observer an explanation of the thought-processes going on. An illustration of this happened where a group of children were working with the basket of fruit and vegetables, and a sorting was being made on whether one ate the skin or not. Onions and bananas caused no difficulties but apples were a source of discussion and compromise. Within any handling of data, this appreciation of the attributes of the data is of key importance.

Some criteria for sorting appear to come far more readily than others. Many children, and indeed adults, will use colour as a first criteria. The shape of the object also comes high on this list and thus one is led to believe that the visual appearance of an object is important. If further sorting criteria are sought, then an attribute that can be counted may be used. For example, with buttons, after sorting into round or square buttons, the number of holes which the buttons possesses is often chosen. For young children, discussion of the reasoning behind their decisions can be helpful, indeed essential, to both teacher and pupil. The children can clarify their own ideas, accepting that some may be quite idiosyncratic, and the teacher can discover what range of criteria the children can use. This discovery may happen either between pupil discussions being overheard informally or through teacher questioning. In many classrooms there will be collections of items which have been commercially produced specifically for sorting activities. In these collections the attributes will be quite distinct – the colours are often primary, the thickness or size is noticeably different and so on. Although these may provide an enjoyable task, the disadvantage of using such collections is that they may have no relevance to other activities going on in the classroom. If there is a topic or theme for much of the work in which the children are involved, then it is a far more useful exercise to bring together collections related to that theme. For example, if toys were a general theme in an infant classroom, a collection of teddies or cars would be complementary and give rise to plenty of sorting with all its associated language.

Early recording activities

Following initial discussions on sorting into different attributes, it is useful to start recording from an early stage. Both Venn and Carroll diagrams (see Figure 7.1) lend themselves to using the actual objects. In a Venn diagram, a loop encloses all the objects possessing an attribute; objects which do not possess it are outside the loop. Young children can find difficulty in expressing the negative idea of not belonging. By discussing how to describe the contents outside of the loop, the naturalness of the situation helps with the introduction of this concept. Large diagrams can be made using sports hoops or skipping ropes; these can be changed to paper recording when appropriate. Labelling of the sets requires care; most texts put the label on the outside of the loop. We think that this could cause confusion and suggest that they should be on the inside (see Figure 7.1a). A useful idea is to use luggage type labels for the labelling to reinforce that this is a label only. It is important to ensure that the children describe clearly what should be on the label to work towards achieving preciseness. Mixing and re-sorting collections and their labels fascinates young children as well as providing both reinforcement and further opportunities for discussion.

Carroll diagrams initially split a set or collection into two parts, one which possesses an attribute and one which does not. Here we support the convention of labelling the two halves, one using the attribute name, and the other with the name crossed out (see Figure 7.1b). One of the major benefits of deciding on this type of labelling is that the language of saying, for example, red and not red, can be well-established before it is met in the context of interrogation of a database. Both Venn and Carroll diagrams and sorting activities can provide excellent practice in the use of *logical connective* words such as *and*, *or* and *not* well before they are used in other areas.

In the early years it is usual to start using horizontal or vertical block graphs to represent information. In some activities it is helpful if each child has their own square to represent themselves – perhaps with their name written on it or a picture they have drawn of themselves. Then, if, for example, they are considering how many brothers and sisters each child has (as part of a family topic) or whose birthdays occur in each month, individuals can add their square to a block graph in the appropriate place. Having a background grid to help with alignment

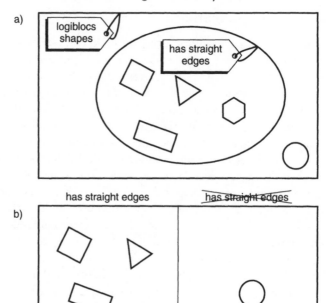

Figure 7.1   Recordings of sorting activities
(a) A Venn diagram for logiblocs.
(b) A Carroll diagram for logiblocs.

will establish the need for a baseline and aid the readability of the graph. These activities provide a sound way into accessing children's thinking and understanding – if they make an error, the question 'why did you put it there?' is immediate. The teacher is instantly presented with the opportunity to act as an *observer*, not as a 'director' of actions. There are computer packages which will produce similar graphs and using them can provide a good introduction to the graphing facilities of a computer. Asking for some brief comments about the graph, for example, the most common number of siblings, can begin to develop the children's interpretations of data, and initiates the second of the two-way process, outlined in the introduction as moving from the abstract back to the concrete.

Throughout these early introductions there are three important threads that need to be borne in mind. First, any work connected with data handling that the children do, is greatly enhanced if it *relates* directly to their own experiences. Second, the opportunities for using *language* to describe the attributes of objects and the sorting need to be exploited whenever possible. Third, the emphasis placed on the *teacher's role* should be one of initiating appropriate activities and then listening and observing, enabling the children to develop their own thinking.

Even as children grow older, the opportunities for sorting may be profitably exploited. There will be a need for rather more complex sorts, perhaps involving two or even three attributes. As an example, consider the following collection of fruits – apple, pear, orange, lemon, banana, kiwi fruit, grapefruit and grape. One of the first considerations is to find the attributes which enable us to distinguish one fruit from another. Possibilities include colour of skin, do we usually eat the skin, sweet or sour, edible seeds, country where they were grown. Clearly some of these divisions are subjective and decisions have to be made about where lines will be drawn – for example, do all children have the same distinction between sweet and sour?

Venn and Carroll diagrams can again be used to incorporate two attributes (see Figure 7.2).

Once more it is worth noting that whilst this type of work could be achieved with commercial materials, the opportunities of bringing mathematical activities into any cross-curricular theme would be lost. One important aspect of these more complex, two attributes diagrams is the use which can be made to illustrate the meanings of *and, or* and *not*. At this stage, it is also possible to introduce sets of more abstract objects to be sorted, for example, numbers. The resulting attribute chosen may well be abstract too – oddness, a multiple of 5, has a 1 as the tens digit. This is a natural developmental step.

Introducing databases

Once the basic ideas of sorting have been understood, the time is right to proceed to work with databases. Indeed, with careful preparation in terms of language when sorting, the complex searching of data can be made easier. A distinction needs to be made between teacher talk and pupil talk. The very meaning of the word *sorting* clearly demonstrates a

a)

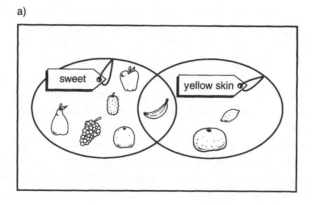

b)   eat the skin   ~~eat the skin~~

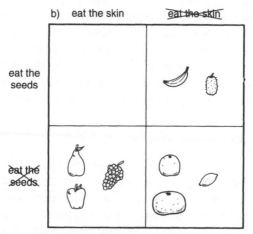

Figure 7.2   Fruit sorted according to its characteristics
(a) A Venn diagram for fruit.
(b) A Carroll diagram for fruit.

quirk of mathematical language. In everyday usage if you asked a group of children to sort themselves out, the meaning is general and thus different from the expectation that in sorting for a database the outcome will be for something specific – the teacher is looking for, say, an alphabetical sort. Sorting in database work will always mean ordering in some (logical) way.

Any collection of information can be thought of as a database. So, for example, a chart in a reception class of the weather on each day of the week is a database. Although this may be mainly pictorial, it could nevertheless give other people a clear idea of what the weather was like over a period of time. Information can be extracted from it – how many days were rainy last week? Have there been more rainy days than sunny days? These types of discussions are building up the ability to ask questions related to information and can provide the children with the opportunity to begin to make some predictions (possibly dangerous with the vagaries of weather in some areas!). Information may be stored in a variety of forms from pictorial illustrations to tables and charts both on paper and, later, in computer programs. Finding out answers to questions that may be relevant is referred to as *interrogating a database*. Children will need to investigate what type of questions they may ask in order to receive appropriate answers, as well as requiring time in learning how to access the responses.

Numerous types of everyday object collections exist which give a great deal of information and can therefore be used as a basis for a database. For example, consider a bus ticket. It has on it the price, the date and the type of ticket (single/return) along with some other coded information relating to the route number, the last fare stage and the number of the ticket machine. If several tickets were collected, the key pieces of information could be displayed in a larger format by mounting on larger card. Questions about the information could then be asked. Were any journeys made in February? What was the least/ most expensive journey? How many return journeys were made? Another excellent source is food packaging and all the information it contains – price, weight, country of origin, nutritional values, etc. Concentration on one particular type of food may be sensible – tinned fruit, beans and pulses, rice, chocolate bars. The general wealth of information contained within such collections and the type of questions which can be asked, provide links to and from other curriculum areas either as a starting point or as an integral part of more general topic work.

Some uniform way of recording the information may well become necessary if this is to be a whole class activity. This in itself can provide a lead into the decision-making that is necessary prior to making a computer database. Children can be involved in the decision-making about what attributes to select and how the results should be displayed in order to make the information clear; this provides another opportunity of 'exposing' children's thinking.

Activities such as those described above are helpful in providing

117

background before actually using a computer. Their value should not be under-rated and time spent on them should help in the *creation* (setting up) and *interrogation* (questioning/searching) of a computer database.

Creating databases

Databases are of two distinct types – ones that use a tree or branching structure and those that do not. A *tree* database uses a series of questions to sub-divide the collection. Returning to the collection of fruit used earlier, an initial question for our fruit might be – do we usually eat the skin? Then the group for which the answer was no (orange, lemon, banana, kiwi, grapefruit) can be split again by another question. Can it be divided into segments? Usually this process is continued until each fruit is alone at the end of a branch. If a new fruit is to be added to the tree, then each question needs to be answered, as it 'moves' from the start and 'proceeds' along the branches, until it is at the top of the tree alongside one other fruit. An additional question can then be devised which will separate the two. With large groups of objects this can be a difficult process but the observational skills that it practices are extensive and by carrying out such activities children are helped in organizing their thinking. A collection of leaves from the school grounds can be a good starting point – smell may be an appropriate attribute here!

All the questions used in sorting these collections have had yes/no answers. Here we see the importance of earlier experiences of sorting and the language involved. The corresponding trees are known as *binary trees*, since a branch splits into two at its end. It is possible either to draw up the tree on paper or to make use of computer software (either looking at the tree on the computer screen or as a printout) or both. One will complement the other depending upon the particular situation. Figure 7.3 shows the type of tree that can be created.

Once the tree has been set up, children can then choose one of the objects and answer the questions to see if they agree (with the computer or with the person who made the drawing), about the name of the object. Using a binary tree is one way of introducing children to new objects – say a new fruit. Trees can be made to include objects such as musical instruments, countries, fiction books, articles of clothing, numbers and so on; another extensive list for cross-curricular links.

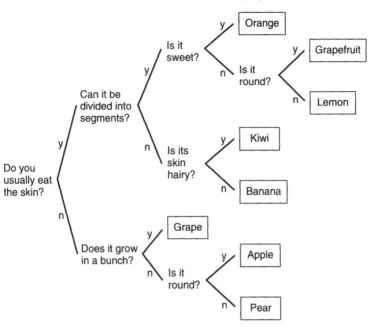

Figure 7.3 A tree diagram for fruit.

Yes/no questions can be used to set up a *punched card* database. Making and using a set of punched cards is a useful way to move on to more sophisticated searching problems involving multiple attributes. Each object has a card with a series of holes along one edge. Each hole refers to one question. If the answer to a particular question is yes the hole is left intact but if the answer is no then the hole is cut open (see Figure 7.4).

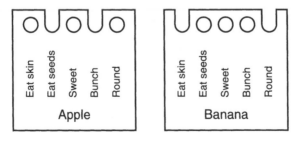

Figure 7.4 Part of a punched card database.

Once all the objects have a card, then it is possible to use these to extract information. If all the objects are required which possess a specific attribute, then a blunt rod passed through the relevant hole of all the cards will 'catch' the cards with that attribute. Indeed this process can be extended to put two rods through simultaneously giving an *or* relation. (Some cards may be swinging on one or other of the rods whilst others having the two attributes will be held on both.) Alternatively, having passed a rod through to extract cards with one attribute (thus discarding those cards which do not), the rod is passed through a second attribute on the selected subset of cards, giving an *and* relation. Constructing such cards give individual children an opportunity to be actively involved in the decisions relevant to the specific characteristics of objects. Such an activity lends itself well to learning names and special characteristics of geometric shapes, e.g. square, rhombus, triangle, and even perhaps prisms etc.

The second type of database is perhaps more common and works in a *file-card* type. Children's thinking is often 'pictorial' and it may help to develop a picture akin to a file-card box (see fig 7.5) when introducing the terminology used with a computer database in its early stages.

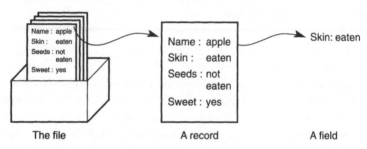

Figure 7.5 The file-card analogy.

Certainly, developing appropriate language is an important part of abstraction. Discussions centred on a set of file-cards (a set of school library cards can be a useful source) is extremely helpful. All the information about an object is called a *record*. Entries corresponding to the attributes are entered into this record. The individual types of attribute are known as *fields*. Each field can be either *alphanumeric* (information like colour or shape in words or words and numbers combined) or *numeric* (numbers only like price or weight). For numeric fields there is often the option to include units for the data. The whole collection of records is a *file*. Whilst children can find difficulty on first meeting some of the terms, it is worth spending time developing the understanding as some software still relies on such terminology as field, record, file, alphanumeric and numeric.

Before discussing how a database may be incorporated into the work in a classroom, one important decision has to be made by the teacher over whether to use an existing datafile or to create a new one. Whatever the decision, it is important to bear in mind that the final goal should be for the children to be able *to use* a database when applicable.

Initial experience can be obtained by working with a file which has already been created; many computer databases have such files available. The main difficulty in using a pre-written file is that the user needs to understand the type of information that has been stored and the way in which it has been entered. If the amount of information on individual objects is not too extensive, then this is much easier. Specific questions can at first be given to the children so that they gain experience of different ways of extracting information, before they progress to asking questions of their own. Working in this way will provide another opportunity for the teacher to observe a child's thinking through the latter's interaction with such a database.

If a new file is to be made, it is helpful if adequate preparatory work has been done in such a way so that the children can make *informed decisions* about the fields to be used, the required number of records and so on. Good planning can often be done sitting at a table, using pencil and paper and without a computer anywhere nearby. Thinking and reflection away from the computer form an integral part of the learning process. A topic with which they are familiar, such as ourselves, homes, people who help us or some collection of real objects can provide a very useful starting point. Each child, or a pair of children, can be responsible for one record. Once decisions have been made and information entered onto the computer, the file is complete and children can find out about the entries of other people and begin the process of interrogation.

Interrogating databases

It is helpful to consider three different approaches to interrogation, each of which complements or supplements the others. Each approach helps children to structure their thinking in different ways. Consider a file on dinosaurs (one piece of software comes with such a file). First, individual records can be *examined* and information about that object *retrieved* (for example – look at the record for the dinosaur called Stegosaurus, what did it eat?). Second, the records can be *sorted* (here the language has changed to mean specific order sorting). The actual sort will depend on the type of field involved. Numeric entries will be sorted numerically (for example – the lengths of the dinosaurs) and others alphabetically (the type of food that the dinosaur ate). Finally, records can be *searched* according to some criterion or criteria (for example – length greater than 6m; lives in water *and* eats plants; lives in water *or* eats plants). It may be possible to discover an answer to a question by several different routes. Each route will reflect a logical progression in step-by-step characterization of the 'object'. Investigating these different routes is all part of the process of database interrogation and of considerable importance when discussing in further work, efficient and logical searching. Increasingly, visual material is being included in commercially produced computer files, and this can greatly enhance the interest and curiosity of the children. Such visual images provide the stimulus for talking about relevant characterization that will form the basis for a database.

Virtually all databases have a graphing facility that brings the possibility of producing good quality pie-charts, bar charts, line graphs or scatter graphs within the reach of all. Some of the graphs would be difficult to produce otherwise. Pie-charts in particular fall into this category; whilst many children will find it almost impossible to construct a pie-chart for themselves without the number of records being a very simple factor of 360, a presented pie-chart can be interpreted by children of differing range in both age and ability. However, it must be said that it is equally possible to produce graphs which are completely meaningless or have no bearing on a particular line of enquiry. This demonstrates that there is a clear need for discussion between the teacher and the children about the graphs which are obtained. It is expedient to expect any child to be able to describe what a graph is illustrating and a piece of written work to accompany a graph aids communication in general.

Using databases in the classroom

In summary, we consider the type of work described in this chapter to be an important part in equipping children from an early age with an appreciation of information and data. Whilst the process of sorting is one which can begin with very young children, we should maintain the ideas throughout the child's education. The ability to pick out relevant attributes has importance not only within mathematics but in science and many of the humanities where such work allows for cross-curricular links to arise naturally. Many books are now published with activities suitable for the primary classroom (see, for example, Davies, 1993) while others provide a more detailed guide to data handling than has been possible in this chapter (Green and Graham, 1994).

Data handling enhances particularly a problem centred approach to teaching mathematics by helping the development of enquiring in a specific context. We have certainly experienced the satisfaction that children show when seeing information about themselves and their interests appearing on a computer screen. Searching a database can give rise to interesting by-products to the primary curriculum. We have appreciated how new vistas have been opened up from such small beginnings as seeing, for example, a scatter graph, or finding a display indicating the median of a set of data, long before it is 'part of the syllabus'. This type of work is equipping our pupils for modern-day life.

REFERENCES

Mann, W. and Tall, D. (1992) *Computers in the Mathematics Curriculum*. London: The Mathematical Association.

Davies, G. (1993) *Practical Data Handling: Book A*. London: Hodder and Stoughton.

Green, D. and Graham, A. (1994) *Data Handling*. Warwickshire: Scholastic.

Shuard, H. and Williams, E. (1994) *Primary Mathematics Today: 4th Edition*. Harlow: Longman.

CHAPTER 8

In Search of the Unknown: A Review of Primary Algebra

ANNIE OWEN

Many modern curriculum recommendations for primary mathematics contain explicit reference to the area of algebra. This has surprised teachers and parents, for whom the word 'algebra' evokes often unhappy memories from the later years of schooling. Episodes of struggling with equations to 'find x', manipulating algebraic fractions and simplifying brackets – all to no apparent purpose and with varying degrees of success – cannot have relevance for young children. So, exactly what is algebra and why is it suddenly important in the primary classroom?

It is difficult to find a definition of algebra which will satisfy all mathematicians, never mind mathematics educators and curriculum developers. A popular description is that of a language for communicating and exploring mathematical relationships and methods of proving such relationships. As we shall see, the way in which the counting numbers (1, 2, 3, 4, etc.) relate and their manipulation through addition, subtraction, etc. is the beginning of studying number properties and a young child's own language for relating what they notice is the beginning of algebraic language.

This chapter will look at the two most common themes of number properties – *number patterns* and *number structure* – and possible routes to formal mathematical language through generalization to functions and equations.

Pattern and structure

The word 'pattern' is over-used in the English language and is, given the variety of contexts in which children meet it, confusing. A child's painting, or a tree bark rubbing, may be described as an 'interesting pattern', but contains no mathematics – no symmetries or no underlying number structure. We speak of the 'pattern of life', meaning its cyclical structure, and of 'patterns of government', meaning a variety of organizational structures. 'Pattern' is also used to mean a template, as in a dress pattern, or a list of instructions, as in a knitting pattern. However, we expect children to understand the meaning of 'mathematical pattern' when in the context of school mathematics. Is this a simple, well-defined concept? Obviously, pattern in shape and pattern in number are easily distinguishable, but within algebra itself, the definition is not so clear. Three types of pattern met at the primary level are: Repeating Patterns, Structural Patterns and Sequences.

REPEATING PATTERNS

Children in the early years are encouraged to recognize, reproduce and finally devise their own repeated patterns using common items such as building blocks, beads, logic shapes, etc.:

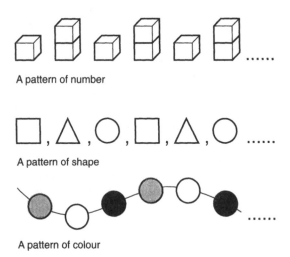

A pattern of number

A pattern of shape

A pattern of colour

Figure 8.1   Patterns in mathematics.

Here, pattern means 'cycle'. Cyclical structures are important in higher mathematics, but there is a more immediate use here for the teacher of 5- to 7-year-olds in the introduction of symbolic representation. Jerome Bruner [1966] stresses the importance of representation as the way in which we manage to order our experiences, moving, as we become more sophisticated, through three modes: the *enactive mode*, where something is learnt by doing it, or by hands-on experience; the *iconic mode*, where an action or object is replaced by an image and the *symbolic mode*, where the child learns to use a code or symbols to represent the action or object.

Mathematical understanding cannot progress without a mastery of its attendant code, and therefore learning to interpret symbols is vital for the 5- to 7-year-old pupil. Repeating patterns provide an ideal vehicle as they are found naturally (e.g. the seasons) and in the man-made environment (e.g. days of the week). The children's own experiences of these cycles provide the enactive mode, pictures and models the iconic mode, and the names for the seasons, the days of the week etc. the symbolic mode. More abstract symbolization is met in several areas of the early years' curriculum. Teachers of music to the early years will already be familiar with using a symbol to stand for an instrument, initially using a picture of the instrument itself, followed by some symbol chosen by the children. This can be expanded to include movement in P.E., and extended by the use of numbers to stand for the number of times the instrument, and/or the movement, is repeated. Such activities prepare children for the formal recording of the patterns they are to meet and to make with numbers.

Activities with repeating patterns also introduce the young child to elements of mathematical thought which are not available to them through any other medium in mathematics. These are: recognition of an event, prediction of a future event, generalization of a rule and communication of that rule. A child who does not yet have a grasp of number beyond five, say, cannot experience such concepts through work with numbers. Repeating patterns made with multilink, beads, music, movement, etc., therefore provide an ideal medium.

STRUCTURAL PATTERNS

Once children begin to explore and manipulate numbers, we meet a different use of the word 'pattern'. For example, how many different ways can you make 5? Can you see a pattern?:

$$4 + 1 = 5$$
$$3 + 2 = 5$$
$$2 + 3 = 5$$
$$1 + 4 = 5$$

Here 'pattern' means structure: How is the number 5 made? What are its properties?

The term 'structure' in mathematics education is also one which has changed with time. Catherine Stern (Stern and Stern, 1953) introduced the teaching of arithmetic through concentration on inter-relationships between numbers rather than through counting. The equipment she developed (Stern apparatus) became known as 'structured apparatus' or 'manipulative aids', terms we now apply to any materials which help children through the transitional stage of iconic representation. Geoffrey Howson (Howson, *et al.*, 1981) refers to the influence of the Bourbaki Project in identifying how the field of mathematics could be build up from a few basic ideas, called 'mother structures'. This project had a direct effect upon our mathematics curriculum, introducing the study of sets, groups and logic at secondary level under the banner 'modern mathematics'. It is interesting to note that today these subjects have all but disappeared in primary mathematics in Britain and the USA and indeed are only to be found as some notional idea of data collection. They also survive for nursery and reception children, where work with sets is seen as a fundamental preliminary to counting.

A further development in mathematics teaching has been that of the 'constructivist' theory of learning discussed in Chapter 1. Children construct their own meanings of mathematical concepts and a mental model of how these concepts interlink. This 'schema' will change when the child meets a phenomenon which directly contradicts it (cognitive conflict). The teacher's role hence becomes that of facilitator, to provide experiences to enable the child to reach their own conclusions and to provide counter-examples when the child's understanding is faulty.

A common theme pervades all these developments – that children cannot expand their understanding of number beyond the repetition of algorithms without an understanding of the underlying structure of number and of number operations. Teachers of primary children therefore need to study these structures, in order to ensure that they provide their pupils with appropriate experiences. Although the children do not meet the formal definitions of these patterns, or rules, it is not enough to assume that they will internalize them and incorporate them into their 'schema'. It is most important that they be stated explicitly in the children's own terms through discussion and writing.

All the patterns and rules discussed in this chapter work for positive whole numbers. Readers may wish to explore for themselves what happens for negative numbers, fractions, and other types of numbers.

127

Structure in Number Operations

Addition The simplest exploration of number structure is that of *partitioning*. Partitioning can be single (the splitting of a number into two smaller numbers) or multiple (a split into several numbers). Children often meet partitioning as the 'story' of a number, in which they find all the ways of splitting that number. For example, the story of five can be explored with counters and with coloured rods. Single partitions of the number five can be shown with one hand. Similarly, ten can be shown with two hands

Children may see patterns in the blocks and hands, for example the symmetry of the patterns for '3 and 7' and '7 and 3'. Formal recording of the results will help them see the structure more clearly:

$$1 + 4 = 5$$
$$2 + 3 = 5$$
$$3 + 2 = 5$$
$$4 + 1 = 5$$

The children may notice – spontaneously, or after a prompt – that the numbers go down one way and up the other. Although this may seem trivial to an adult, to a child this may be a revelation. Also, there is symmetry about the table of results as a whole. That $1 + 4$ is the same as $4 + 1$ illustrates an important property of addition – the *commutative* property (or 'commutativity'). Many mental methods of calculation depend upon this knowledge. For example, young children will, if asked to find $2 + 8$ begin at the 2 and add – usually on fingers – up to the 8. This is time consuming and there are many opportunities to go wrong. Only later will they realize that they can begin at the 8 and add 2 and get the same answer. Experimenting with partitions, as above, can help children make these connections more quickly.

Partitioning can also be multiple, for example:

$$5 = 1 + 1 + 1 + 1 + 1$$
$$5 = 2 + 1 + 1 + 1$$
$$5 = 2 + 2 + 1 \text{ etc.}$$

This leads us on to another rule obeyed by addition, the *associative* rule: taking $5 = 3 + 1 + 1$ does it matter whether we add the 3 and 1 first and then the other 1, or if we add the two 1s and then add them to the 3?

$$(3 + 1) + 1 = 3 + (1 + 1)$$

Children who realize that it *doesn't* matter can choose how to do the sum. For most of us, adding the two ones first is easier, as doubling is one of the most natural of arithmetic processes. Again, this knowledge provides us with flexibility in mental calculation.

Older children, and adults, with quick and successful mental methods use such knowledge to find sophisticated short-cuts. For example, in adding 27 and 45: one common method is to look for a 'complement' of 45, i.e. a number which we can add to 45 to make a multiple of 10. Some will use 5, make 50 and then add on the remaining 22 (adding on to multiples of 10 being easier):

$$27 + 45 = 22 + 50 = 72$$

Others will add 3 to the 27 to make 30:

$$27 + 45 = 30 + 42 = 72$$

Many will begin with the 45, adding on 10, then 10 then 7, secure in the knowledge that it doesn't matter which number you begin with. All these methods depend upon the commutativity and associativity of addition.

Multiplication   It is not surprising that, given our model of multiplication as repeated addition, multiplication obeys the same rules. Multiplication is commutative, for example: $3 \times 5 = 15$ and $5 \times 3 = 15$. Multiplication is associative, for example: $(2 \times 3) \times 4 = 2 \times (3 \times 4) = 24$. The answer is the same whether you first do 2×3 and then multiply by 4, or multiply 2 by 3×4.

Subtraction and Division   Through exploration using structured apparatus or calculators, we can help children to understand that subtraction *isn't* commutative (the word is not important, only the idea), for example while 7 equals $9 - 2$, it doesn't equal $2 - 9$. Interestingly, if children try this on a calculator, they will get -7, which they will 'feel' is the same in some way, and we are into the world of negative numbers.

Neither is subtraction associative. If we take the sum: $9 - 5 - 2$, the answer will depend upon which subtraction is done first. $(9 - 5) - 2 = 2$ but $9 - (5 - 2) = 6$.

However, subtraction does follow some patterns: e.g. $9 - 2 = 7$ and

$9 - 7 = 2$. We shall call this the 'swap' rule. The swap rule is not one of the fundamental rules of arithmetic (like commutativity and associativity) but is a consequence of the other rules. Recognition of such patterns offers children a chance to mentally check their answers.

Division, often modelled as repeated subtraction, behaves in the same way: division is *not* commutative: $15 \div 3 = 5$ but $3 \div 15$ gives a different answer. Division is *not* associative: $(20 \div 2) \div 5 = 2$, $20 \div (2 \div 5) = 50$. Like subtraction, division does obey the swap rule: $15 \div 3 = 5$ and $15 \div 5 = 3$.

A further rule for multiplication and division is the *distributive* rule: Take $8 \times 4 = 32$. The 8 can be split into $3 + 5$. To find 8 lots of 4 we can add 3 lots of 4 and 5 lots of 4 to get 32:

$$8 \times 4 = (5 + 3) \times 4 = (5 \times 4) + (3 \times 4)$$

The distributive rule also holds for division:

$$18 \div 3 = (12 + 6) \div 3 = (12 \div 3) + (6 \div 3) = 6$$

The distributive rule is important when children come to work with larger numbers. For example, to multiply 7 by 13:

$$7 \times 13 = 7 \times (10 + 3) = 7 \times 10 + 7 \times 3 = 70 + 21 = 91$$

Standard algorithms for long multiplication all depend upon this 'splitting' of numbers into more manageable elements (tens and units, or hundreds, tens and units).

Another important concept in the structure of number is the *inverse* of an operation. That addition and subtraction are inverses of each other (similarly multiplication and division) is fundamental for the solution to such problems as $4 + ? = 13$. It can be solved by 'adding on', but children will become more proficient if they realize that they can also do a subtraction.

Finally, a system is *closed* under an operation if all the answers still belong to the system. We have been dealing here with positive whole numbers. If a positive whole number is added to a positive whole number, will you always get a positive whole number? What about subtraction? Division? Children meeting odd and even numbers are often asked such questions – does an odd number plus an odd number make another odd number?

The names for the rules above are unimportant to the children. The concepts, though, are vital both for improving mental mathematics and for their future development in algebra. To summarize them with symbolic notation (not for pupil consumption!):

Commutative rule: a*b = b*a (applies to addition, multiplication)

Associative rule: a*(b*c) = (a*b)*c (applies to addition, multiplication)

Swap rule: if a*b = c then a*c = b (applies to subtraction, division)

Distributive rule: if a*b = c and a = d + e
then (d + e)*b = d*b + e*b = c (applies to multiplication, division)

SEQUENCES

A sequence, in the school context, is a non-repeating list of numbers which are generated by following a rule like 5, 10, 15, 20 (begin at 5 and add 5) ... or 14, 24, 34, ... (begin at 14 and add 10). Unfortunately, everyday language uses the word differently (a dance sequence is often a repeating pattern). Sequences are part of the building blocks of mathematical analysis, with which we can predict the final outcome of observed phenomena in science, engineering and statistics. For example, the calculation of market trends is dependent upon the analysis of the sequence the market appears to be following. People working with sequences need to be able to recognize patterns of growth in the numbers or use techniques of analysis to investigate them. Computer packages now exist to speed up such calculation, but it must be remembered that someone has to write the program!

As so many sequences grow out of games and puzzles – so-called 'recreational mathematics' – this work has the advantage of enticing children to think about number and to practice computation in an interesting way. Problem solving skills are enhanced and children may also discover new ways of looking at numbers. Look, for example, at the sequence made by adding consecutive odd numbers:

$$1 = 1$$
$$1 + 3 = 4$$
$$1 + 3 + 5 = 9$$
$$1 + 3 + 5 + 7 = 16$$

Why do we get square numbers? Modelling with counters or multilink can show the relationship.

131

Generalization and proof

If a statement can be made about the pattern involved in some number relationship or in a sequence, so that predictions can be made about further numbers, then that statement is a generalization. For example, if a 6-year-old tries adding odd and even numbers and finds that in all the cases she has tried an odd + an odd = an even, then she can make a *generalization* that this will always happen and then check with further examples (a good strategy is to ask the rest of the group to try to prove she is wrong!). She can never be *absolutely* sure that the statement is correct until she is of an age to study mathematical proof. Apart from the travails of Euclidean proof, to which readers of my own age and over were subjected while studying for examinations, proof has been very much in the realm of advanced mathematics. However, as open-ended tasks have been introduced, and as children have begun to describe generalizations for the sequences or relationships they have discovered, the need to know 'for sure' if their conclusions are correct has meant that the need for proof has begun to trickle down to the primary classroom. Obviously, children who are not yet able to use algebraic expressions cannot ever construct a proof which would be deserving of the name to a pure mathematician, but there are three fundamental concepts which *are* within the grasp of primary children and which are initial building blocks to understanding proof.

First, children need to realize that they can never be sure what will come next in a sequence unless they know the rule for that sequence. Building up a sequence bit by bit illustrates this concept well:

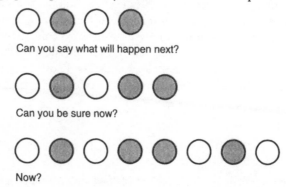

Can you say what will happen next?

Can you be sure now?

Now?

Figure 8.2 Investigating patterns.

132

If children share their ideas and say why they think their guess is correct, then the group can come to see that there are many possibilities and any of them could be right. However, the only way to be *really* sure how a pattern will continue is to know what the maker of the pattern is thinking! In other words, you need to know the '*rule*'.

Second, children should appreciate that a guess at a rule is completely wrong if just one example can be found which contradicts, that is doesn't fit the guess. For example, children investigating prime numbers beyond 3 may quickly reach the conclusion that primes bigger than 3 always come in pairs: 5 and 7, 11 and 13, 17 and 19. However, it only takes one example, e.g. 23, which stands alone, to disprove this generalization. This is called a *counter-example* and shows the suggested rule is not correct.

Finally, explaining why a sequence grows the way it does, or why some numbers behave the way they do, is well on the way to a formal proof. To illustrate, let us return to our statement: an odd number + an odd number = an even number. An odd number of objects can always be arranged in twos with one left over. If two odd numbers are put together, then the two 'leftover' objects will make another pair and we *must* get an even number.

Alternatively, take the problem of the garden pond:

Put a path around a square fish pond:
How many paving stones do you need?
What about a bigger pond (keep it square)?
Continue making paths for larger ponds.

This problem generates the sequence: 8, 12, 16, 20, 24. Many 6-year-olds can recognize this pattern, can describe it to you and can continue it, but far fewer can tell you why the sequence goes up in fours. Many 9- to 11-year-olds can see that the sequence goes up in fours because, as the square grows in side length by one, a gap of one paving stone appears in *each* of the four sides, and therefore they can be sure that the numbers will continue to grow in this way. Such proof was completely acceptable to the ancient Greeks (who had no algebra) and this method of thinking – looking at the changes produced at each stage – forms the basis of the more modern 'proof by induction'. In the primary classroom, we only wish for children to think 'But why do we get that?' However, in doing so, we equip them for more complex justifications later on.

Functions and equations

In mathematical terms, a *function* is a special relation in which every element in one set of numbers is assigned to one and only one element in another set of numbers. The concept of a function is too abstract for young children to grasp unless they are given an object on which to focus which is responsible for the change. The progress towards greater abstraction can be compared to Bruner's three modes: *enactive, iconic* and *symbolic*. At the enactive level, this may be a curtain which, when a child walks behind it, a hat is put on her head. Everyone walking behind gets a hat, and 'getting a hat' is the function or 'change' which comes about. Games such as 'Simple Simon Says', where everyone reacts in some way to an instruction are also enactive function activities. The distinction between enactive and iconic, and iconic and symbolic, is not so clear-cut, though we can pinpoint progression in the level of abstraction moving towards the stage of understanding notation such as: $n \rightarrow 3n + 1$.

For example, instead of large-scale movement by the children, imagine a box which changes objects fed into it. Logic blocks are useful materials, as they can change by four attributes: colour, size, shape or thickness. The teacher stands behind a real box, or 'function machine', with the logic pieces inside, and feeds pieces in and out. Real pieces can be replaced by pictures of logiblocks or other objects, followed by recording in pictorial (iconic) form.

A more advanced activity is the replacement of the machine box with a picture of one followed by a diagrammatic representation of one (see Figure 8.3a). Similarly, this increasingly abstract sequence can be enacted for numbers (see Figure 8.3b). The *function* then is 'add 2' and can be recorded in a way recognizable to younger pupils (see Figure 8.3c).

That a fundamental element of algebra which underlies what the children are doing is of no interest whatsoever to them, but it *is* important that we as teachers realize that such work prepares children for the time when they will generate sequences for themselves.

Any pair of numbers, for example 6 and 8, can be taken from such a mapping and written formally with the function thus: $6 + 2 = 8$; which provides the first type of equation met by young children. Usually we present them with missing elements in order to check children's

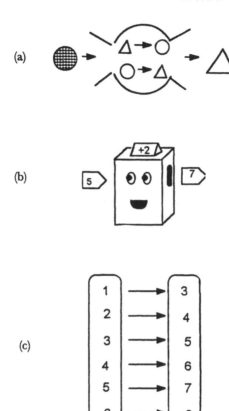

Figure 8.3   Illustrations of mathematical functions
(a) Illustrating a mathematical function
(b) Illustrating the function 'add 2'
(c) Different ways of indicating the function 'add 2'

understanding of arithmetic processes, or to provide practice. $3 + 4 = \square$ presents little difficulty to a child who can interpret the symbols, can count and who understands simple addition. However, the introduction of an unknown elsewhere can be very problematic in such problems as $3 + \square = 7$ or $\square + 4 = 7$.

Again, the use of an object to provide focus can help children to interpret the question:

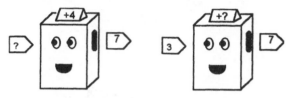

Figure 8.4   Function machines.

My machine adds four. If seven comes out, what went in? Three goes in and seven comes out. What is my machine adding?

Children who solve the problem can come to understand that addition and subtraction are inverses operations. How operations are connected, for example that repeated addition gives the same results as multiplication, that repeated subtraction gives the same result as division, or that multiplication and division are inverses of each other, enables children to build up for themselves a picture or 'schema' of how operations 'behave' and hence to find their own strategies for solving number problems.

Symbolic representation

Children solving equations such as $3 + \square = 10$, or playing a game where tokens are exchanged for 10s in a place-value game, can already accept that a symbol or an object can stand for a number. They can visualize the simple substitution of a number into the box, or ten units in place of the token. However, once manipulation of symbols involves more than one operation, for example $2 \times \mathbf{n} + 3 = 11$, visualization becomes much more difficult. Many 9- to 11-year-olds can solve such equations if they are assisted with certain strategies. Three methods described here are the 'cover up' method, the 'function machine' method and the 'balance' method. These methods have developed from work with secondary pupils, and the problems children of this age have encountered have been well documented in the CSMS report by Lesley Booth (1984). Unfortunately, no such study of errors exists for the primary-aged pupil, but hopefully my own conversations with a class of 10-year-olds will illustrate some of the difficulties – and also some of the surprising abilities – of this age group. At each stage of this work, I asked the children to try to solve a problem first, and then tell the rest of the group how they did it. For each group of children I shall begin with a description of their abilities with simpler equations, to put the subsequent writing in context for the reader.

Andrew, Anne, David and Mark are low-attaining pupils mathematically. David has extra help each day with both mathematics and English. All can solve such equations as $2 + \square = 11$, although their methods vary from counting on, to combination of known facts to 10 with counting. Interestingly, David was the only child to use the inverse function: 'I knew $11 - 1 = 10$, but it had to be 2, so $10 - 1 = 9$'. All four children can use trial-and-improve methods to solve an equation such as: $3 \times \square = 45$, David and Andrew carried out 15 additions of 3, showing an understanding of multiplication as repeated addition. Anne and Mark show the same understanding, but more sophistication.

Anne: '$10 \times 5 = 50$, -5 gives 45 so it must be 9'

Mark: 'If higher than 30, you can take out a 10. 30 plus what equals 45? I know that's 15. Then you get 5. $5 + 10 = 15$'

Presented with their first ever 'compound' equation $\square \times 5 + 10 = 50$, both Andrew and Anne used trial and improve methods, Anne beginning at 5 and Andrew making an initial estimate of 9 followed by a correction.

David: '$50 - 10 = 40$. I want something times 5 is 40'
[David needed help with the arithmetic to get the final answer]

Mark: '10 plus what equals 50. That makes 40. I know $4 \times 10 = 40$, but the ten should be a five, so I doubled the 4. So $8 \times 5 = 40$. The answer is 8.'

I find it amazing that children of supposedly limited mathematical ability can both construct these convoluted methods *and* keep a track of where they are in the calculation!

In the last example, David and Mark are displaying naturally the first strategy which we can show children for solutions of equations where the unknown element occurs only once:

THE 'COVER UP' METHOD

Put your finger over the part you don't know, and the bits nearest to it, so that only one other 'bit' is on the same side:

$$\square \times 5 + 10 = 50$$

$$+ 10 = 50$$

Figure 8.5   The 'cover up' method for solving equations.

What are we hiding? Something plus 10 makes 50. What is the 'something'? Children will use their own methods to reach the answer 40. Rewrite the problem: $\square \times 5 = 40$. Put your finger over the part you don't know, and the bits nearest to it, so that only one other 'bit' is on the same side:

What are we hiding? Something times 5 makes 40. What is the 'something'? Children will use their own methods to reach the answer 8.

This method is helpful when the unknown element isn't at the front of the equation, as in $20 + 2 \times \square = 90$. The low-attaining group of children had not been shown the 'cover up' method. Both David and Andrew began by adding 20 and 2 and then trying to find how many 22s make 90.

Mark: 'Can you divide by 2?'

Annie: 'No' [not the most helpful of responses!]

Mark: 'Can you divide by 20?'

Annie: 'Why divide?'

Mark: 'Oh! No. It's take away.'

Meanwhile, David had rethought the problem.

David: 'If you keep adding 2 up to 70, would that be right?'

[David had difficulty explaining where he got the 70 from. Mark had been listening]

Mark: 'If I'd known it was 70 I could have halved it.'

Anne meanwhile had worked out $90 - 20 = 70$ and wanted $70 \div 2$. This she did by trial and improve and doubling: $20 \rightarrow 40$, $25 \rightarrow 50$, $30 \rightarrow 60$, $35 \rightarrow 70$. The 'cover up' method avoids these problems. Put your finger over the part you don't know, and the bits nearest to it, so that only one other 'bit' is on the same side:

$$20 + 2 \times \square = 90$$

$$20 + = 90$$

Figure 8.6 Using the 'cover up' method.

What are we hiding? Twenty plus something makes 90. What is the 'something'? Children will use their own methods to reach the answer 70. Rewrite the question: $2 \times \square = 70$. Put your finger over the part you don't know, and the bits nearest to it, so that only one other 'bit' is on the same side:

What are we hiding? Two times something makes 70. What is the 'something'? Children will use their own methods to reach the answer 35.

The 'cover up' method is quick and easy to carry out but it has its drawbacks. Children may cover up the wrong 'bits'. For example, in the problem $10 + \square \times 3$ a child may cover up $10 + \square$ instead of $\square \times 3$. This leads to the calculation $? \times 3 = 37$ instead of the required $10 + ? = 37$. One might guess that something is wrong from the answer of 12.333333, though equations don't always turn out with nice whole number answers – especially if the children are making up their own for others to solve. To avoid errors like this, we need to show the children the differences that the order in which an equation is worked can make. Comparing how arithmetic-logic and algebraic-logic calculators work is an excellent illustration.

Arithmetic-logic calculators carry out operations in the order in which they are entered. For example: 20 + 2 × 35 = . The calculator will work out: 20 + 2 = 22, 22 × 35 = 770. Many calculators used in the lower primary years have arithmetic logic.

Algebraic-logic calculators carry out operations in the order: powers, multiplication and division, addition and subtraction. Such calculators will work out: 2 × 35 = 70, 20 + 70 = 90. Many calculators used in the upper primary years, and all 'scientific' calculators have algebraic logic.

It is interesting to give children both calculators and ask them to compare answers to such equations. How could they get the algebraic-logic calculator to do the addition first? Keying in 20 + 2 = × 35 = is one way, but this is a good opportunity to introduce the use of brackets: (20 + 2) × 35 = will give 770.

THE FUNCTION MACHINE METHOD

The equation 3 × □ + 1 = 10 contains two functions: 'multiplying by 3' and 'adding 1'.

The equation can be built up using a 'machine' to represent each function. As stated previously, this helps children cope with an abstraction by giving them a focus for the changes.

Figure 8.7   Abstract function machines.

Children can trace the passage of a starting number through the two machines and draw up a table of results:

IN	OUT
1	4
2	7
3	10
4	13
5	16

The solution to 3 × □ + 1 = 10 can therefore be found using

trial-and-improve through the two machines. However, this will quickly become tedious for the more able pupil, and the idea of working backwards through the machines, if the children haven't thought of it themselves, should be introduced.

Ten can come out of the second machine. This machine made 10 by adding 1 – what should we do to find what went in?

Nine came out of the first machine. This machine made 9 by multiplying by 3 – what should we do to find what went in?

None of my lower ability pupils had difficulty with these concepts. However, what *did* cause problems was the setting up of machine pictures if the original equation was not presented with the unknown at the front. For example, they could cope with: $4 \times \square - 1 = 11$ drawing two machines, the first multiplying by 4 the second subtracting 1. However: $5 + 3 \times \square = 23$ led them to draw an 'add' 5 machine first, and get very confused as to where the unknown went in! We again have the difficulty of the children needing to understand the hierarchy of operations (mentioned under the 'cover up' method). We need to know which function in an equation comes first in order to build up the machines in the right order. Many children who *can* cope with solving simple equations cannot cope with this order problem, and further work in equations needs to be put on hold.

A further difficulty with the machine method, and one I have not tried with primary children, is how to solve an equation where the unknown is being 'taken away from' something, for example $30 - 2 \times \square = 8$. Readers may wish to try to draw a machine combination for this – it isn't easy! However, my low-attaining pupils thought the machine method better than the 'cover up' method because it:

a) Looks nicer, and
b) The problem can be opened out (by which they mean that you can see all the stages in one go, rather than 'forgetting' some for a while)

They worried, though that it:

c) Took up too much space in their books, and
d) It took too long to draw the machines.

Alex, Faye, Martin and Simon are a middle-ability group in the same class. All can solve equations such as: $2 \times \square + 5 = 13$. All can use the 'standard' method: $13 - 5 = 8$, $2 \times 4 = 8$, though they sometimes choose trial-and-improve or more round-about methods. This group have met function machines, but do not need them – they can visualize an equation where there is only one unknown.

I wanted to introduce this group to equations with more than one unknown, and the balance method. However, I thought it better to tidy up the equations by introducing a letter instead of $\square$, and removing the $\times$ sign: $2n + 7 = 16$

Simon: But that's impossible!

Annie: Why?

Simon: Twenty-something plus 7 can't be 16.

Martin: 16 is less than 10. It can't go.

All four children saw the **n** as standing for a unit number, with the 2 taking the 'tens' value. $2n$ is therefore 20 plus **n**. However, an explanation soon cleared the matter, only Faye repeating the mistake and she also eventually understood.

When presented with the equation $3n + 7 = 2n + 15$, this group of children found it very difficult to understand that the two 'somethings' on either side of the equation stood for the same number. They were in need of help in visualization. The balance method was therefore introduced.

THE BALANCE METHOD

An equation can be thought of as a system in 'balance' with the two sides 'weighing' the same. This visualization is not new to teachers of 5- to 7-year-olds, who use both equalizers and weighing scales to model number work. For example, the equation $3 + \square = 7$ can be modelled on an equalizer balance with the number 3 on one side and the number 7 outweighing it on the other, the child finding a solution by adding different numbers through trial-and-improve. Alternatively, weights (e.g. multilink cubes) can be placed in scale pans, 3 on one side and 7 on the other, the children then finding how many must be added to 3 to balance.

An equation such as $5 + 3 \times \square = 23$ can be solved by modelling the balanced equation as though on a scales. Imagine the $\square$ as a box containing an unknown number of counters. We want to know what is inside the $\square$ (the box). Therefore we need to have only the $\square$ on the left-hand side. If we take away the 5, the scales won't balance any more, so we must take 5 away from the right-hand side at the same time to get $3 \times \square = 18$.

Now we know that three lots of whatever is in the box weighs the same as 18. Therefore the box must contain 6.

This will strike a chord with many teachers, who learnt by heart 'whatever you do to one side, you must do to the other'. The final stage, of dividing both sides by 3, is missing, but then we all too often ask pupils to continue a process long after they can see the answer. Following an algorithm beyond the point at which it is necessary only undervalues the child's intellect.

The middle-ability group of children needed one extra stage in this visualization – $3 \times \square$ needed to initially be replaced by three little boxes $\square\square\square$. All four could then carry out the manipulations, Martin doing them in his head. However, look closely at the following example:

$$6n + 7 = 9n + 28$$

Martin: $28 - 7 = 21$. Three extra bags. $3 \times 7 = 21$, so the answer must be 7

Faye reached the same conclusion, while Alex and Simon struggled not surprisingly as a closer look at the equation will reveal that it is impossible for positive numbers. (I produced this example by accident, though the mistake was quite fortuitous!) The children had learnt the method well, but in cutting corners Martin and Faye lost the meaning.

Finally, let us look at how the most able four pupils in this class, Felicity, Ian, Steven and William, cope with equations. All four children could solve simple equations such as $3 + \square = 8$ and $30 \div \square = 6$ with no hesitation. The three boys used known addition and multi-plication bonds, whereas Felicity resorted to more 'round about' methods. When given the equation $2n + 5 = 17$ (the children had already met the idea that $2n$ meant $2 \times n$) all three boys worked out $17 - 5 = 12$, $12 \div 2 = 6$. Felicity worked through: $7 - 5 = 2$, $2 + 10 = 12$, half of 12 is 6. Once reminded what a bracket can do, all four children could solve: $2(3 + n) = 24$ all using $24 \div 2 = 12$, the boys working $12 - 3 = 9$, Felicity asking herself $3 + ? = 12$, then trial-and-improve.

These children therefore appeared ready to begin looking at equations where the unknown appears on both sides of the equation, and for which neither the 'cover up' nor the 'function machine' methods would be of help. I gave them: $n + 6 = 3n$.

- Felicity used trial-and-improve
- Ian who ... knew it must be below 6, because $18 > 12$ and multiplying goes up faster than adding used trial-and-improve with numbers below 6.
- Steven could just see it!
- William saw that $3 = 6 = 9$ and $3 \times 3 = 9$, but knew this wouldn't work for bigger numbers.

I next set the problem $2n + 7 = 3n$. This proved very difficult. The children made little headway, though Steven did comment that 2x anything must be even and so 2x anything plus 7 must be odd. I explained the balance method (though not very well!): [starting with $2n + 7$ in one pan and $3n$ in the other pan so that the pans balance]

Annie: What could I remove, and the scales still balance?

Felicity: Take an n from each side? But if you do, you'll have $9 = 3$!

Felicity obviously had difficulty with this method when the equation was written in the standard form $2n$ rather than $2 \times n$.

Reminding Felicity what $2n$ meant, we continued: $5n + 15 = 8n$

Steven: $8n - 5n = 3n$
$15 = 3n$
$n = 5$ [Steven drew a scale balance]

William: 15 must equal $3n$
$3 \times 5 = 15$, so $n = 5$ [William drew a scale balance]

Ian: worked the problem as above, but did not draw a balance.

Felicity: used trial-and-improve and was obviously most unhappy about the balancing method.

To help Felicity, I returned to the 'box' analogy. In the left side of the balance are five boxes plus fifteen counters. In the right side are eight boxes. All the boxes have the same number of counters in them. What is that number?

This visualization provided the clue which helped Felicity to understand the meaning of the equation. She was then able to continue solving such equations with success. All four children quickly found the drawing of balances unnecessary.

The children came unstuck with the following: $2(9 + 3\mathbf{n}) = 12\mathbf{n}$.

Felicity and Ian: $9 + 3 = 12$, so **n** must be 2

Steven: Take three **n** from each side: $2(9) = 9\mathbf{n}$
$$18 = 9\mathbf{n}$$
$$2 = \mathbf{n}$$

William: $2 \times 9 = 18$, which is 6 more than $12\mathbf{n}$, so it looks like **n** is 2
$$2(9 + 6) = 24$$
$$18 + 6 = 24, \text{ so my answer looks right.}$$
[So much for checking your solutions!]

Although the children understood the use of brackets, and all now understood the meaning of $3\mathbf{n}$ the combination of these elements was beyond them. This appeared to be yet again a visualization problem: If we think of the brackets as a shoebox, then on the left-hand side we have two shoeboxes. Inside each shoebox are nine counters and three matchboxes. Inside each matchbox are the same number (**n**) of counters. All this balances with twelve matchboxes on the other side.

The children were able to cope with this explanation – two shoeboxes makes twelve matchboxes, so one shoebox makes six matchboxes. Nine counters plus three matchboxes makes twelve matchboxes, so nine counters makes nine matchboxes. Therefore, there is only one counter in each box (phew!). However, they could not reconstruct this model for similar equations. We had reached the limit of their powers of abstraction.

The other use of abstract symbolization met with children working at the 'top' level of the primary school is the description of sequences in the form of the 'nth term'.

As described earlier in this chapter, very young children can explain how a sequence grows using their own language. For example, 1, 4, 7, 10, 13, 16 'goes up in threes' or 'adds 3 each time'. This is called the 'iterative' description of a sequence. A child who has found an iterative description can continue the pattern as far as the arithmetic skills are available (obviously greatly extended with the use of a calculator) or the patience lasts. Different children may see different iterative descriptions, as in the 'triangle' numbers below.

Build triangles with paper cups:

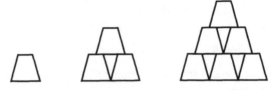

Figure 8.8   Triangular numbers illustrated.
Build triangles with paper cups.

How many cups will we need for the next triangle? the one after that? the 10th one? If we build up a table, we may see a pattern:

Triangle	Number of cups (the triangle number)
1	1
2	3
3	6
4	10
5	15

This may be described as 'the number you add on goes up 1 each time' or ' you add on the triangle you've reached to the last number of cups you got' [for the fifth triangle, add 5 to the last number of cups, 10] or 'you add the two numbers on the line above, plus 1'.

All are correct. However, if we want to know, for example, the 100th triangle number, it would be tedious, time-consuming and prone to error to have to work it out using an iterative description. Nine to 11-year-olds should be encouraged to look for a way to connect where we are in a sequence to the answer. For example, in 1, 4, 7, 10, 13 – the first is 1, the second is 4, the third is 7, the fourth is 10. What do we do to 4 to get 10, so that if we do the same to 3 we get 7, or to 1 we get 1. etc. An explanation such as 'times the number by 3, then take 2' is perfectly acceptable and gives the child the possibility of working out the 100th one: $100 \rightarrow 100 \times 3 - 2 \rightarrow 298$. Children like Felicity, Ian, Steven and William can write this generalization in symbolic form: $3\mathbf{n} - 2$.

Moving children towards symbolization will be more successful if there is some motivation to do so. Exploring sequences with a spreadsheet, or by writing a short computer program, provides an excellent vehicle and readers may wish to read about such work undertaken with secondary pupils by Rosamund Sutherland (1990).

Conclusion

The mathematics with which this chapter has ended begins to look like the algebra most readers will remember from their own school days, where the emphasis is on 'finding x' or describing mathematics in terms of 'x'. It is tempting to call this 'real' algebra and the earlier levels 'pre-algebra', in the mistaken belief that *this* is what is used in the real world of the mathematician or scientist. However, the world of higher mathematics is changing as a result of the increasing power of computer calculation.

Scientists and engineers are increasingly using computer modelling packages in their work and this is influencing higher education courses, where the emphasis is shifting from calculation to interpretation. Increasingly the skills required in adult life are those of experimentation, recognition, application and communication. The algebraic experiences we provide the primary pupil will be an excellent preparation.

REFERENCES

Bruner, J., Oliver, R. R. and Greenfield, P. M. (1966) *Studies in Cognitive Growth.* New York: Wiley.
Howson, G., Keitel, C. and Kilpatrick, J. (1981) *Curriculum Development in Mathematics.* Cambridge: Cambridge University Press.
Stern, C. and Stern, M. B. (1953) *Children Discover Arithmetic.* London: Harrap.

CHAPTER 9

Re-solving Problem Solving

LYNDON BAKER

It is sometimes claimed that problem-solving is at the heart of all mathematics. Certainly school curricula are formulated to reflect the importance of tackling problems in a variety of contexts, situations and formats in the mathematics classroom.

> An individual's future uses and needs for mathematics makes the ability to think, reason, and solve problems a primary goal for the study of mathematics. (NCTM, 1989, p. 18)

But what are appropriate problems for children to tackle? What is the mathematics that they will encounter and how can a teacher 'manage' mathematical learning in a problem-solving environment?

This chapter gives accounts of some episodes with student, pupils and practising teachers working on problem solving and addressing some of the issues that are involved when adopting such an approach to mathematics teaching and learning.

What is problem solving in mathematics?

When considering useful ways in which to enhance children's thinking with relation to the wider skills involved in problem solving it is useful to first consider the perceptions that some teachers have of problem solving. As teachers we usually foster and nurture those elements that we ourselves most value. At the same time, don't children, while trying to achieve success, try to align their ways of working to those they think their teachers will value?

> A group of teachers were asked to think of problems which they had recently met in their everyday lives and to focus on the processes involved in solving them.

Discussion ensued, there was much sharing of experiences; common ground was quickly established; surprise was genuinely felt at the broad range of skills they had accumulated. There was also wholesale agreement about the way in which personal levels of confidence could be enhanced or destroyed depending on the quality of experience and activity undertaken.

A wide range of personal, day-to-day types of experiences had been shared. The teachers had gained much insight with which to next consider:

'What is problem solving in mathematics?'

Some of the processes the teachers mentioned were:

... being able to think beyond the basic skills, being able to use basic skills in different directions and unfamiliar situations
... using mathematical knowledge to unravel and interpret various situations ... adapting knowledge to find out more and sort out a situation
... using mathematics to come to terms with everyday situations
... looking and thinking beyond the literal
... where the answer does not immediately jump out at you, you have to apply mathematical knowledge and skills to try and reach a possible solution
... using skills with confidence and competence to gain a solution ... to gain additional information, thus developing and extending skills
... opportunities to try different approaches to something ... to use existing mathematical skills in context
... having the skill to cope with confidence of others and without being phased, applying knowledge to new situations
... having the ability to apply acquired mathematical skills to relevant problems in order to arrive at a satisfactory conclusion
... finding solutions/possibilities when faced with unfamiliar situations
... having the ability to use previously acquired knowledge and skills to new and unfamiliar situations

The lack of comment about mathematical knowledge *per se* reinforces the issue that the product is subordinated by the process involved. None of the teachers had recognized that any process undertaken often involves an emotional commitment. They were soon to find this out. After coffee a problem was given that was to give a framework to these points of view:

Problem:

Consider a 3 by 3 array consisting of nine 1 by 1 squares on a grid of squared paper.
Colour the outside edges RED.
Now rearrange the nine squares, without turning them over, so that the red edges are no longer on the outside and colour the new outside edges YELLOW.
Can you now rearrange the squares so that both the red and yellow edges are no longer on the outside and colour the remaining outside edges GREEN?

Extend this problem to larger arrays of 1 by 1 squares ... 16, 25, 36, ...

The problem had been chosen because it required a hands-on approach, it suited collaborative work and allowed members of the group to enter the problem easily, irrespective of their mathematical background. These criteria have been found useful when selecting problems for use in the schoolroom when working with children.

That morning the invitation had been for the group to:

- discuss and reach an understanding of the problem;
- investigate further;
- record whatever they found;
- extend the problem (where possible);
- tabulate any results and observations obtained.

Initially there was much commotion as individual teachers sorted materials with which to start the problem. Then a period of calm, as the problem was re-read, clues for an opening (an answer?) were searched for and tentative forays into the problem began. Square pieces of card were soon discarded in favour of paper carefully ripped to a manageable size as the first passages through the problem had proved difficult with no group being able to achieve the green edging.

Disbelief and suggestions that the problem could not be done were all too evident. With a tinge of reluctance all the group returned to the task and more waves of frustration were met. Whispers aside about the difficulties met were overtaken with stronger voices worrying about the relevance of such problems:

Who needs to do anything like this anyway?

My class wouldn't be able to do this, so what's the point?

As well as declarations of personal insecurity:

I could never do problems like these!
I was never good at maths!
No-one showed me how to do things like this!

It was a lone voice that exclaimed:

I think it can be done!

Invited to share her insights to the problem both with her partner on the activity and the group at large, one teacher tentatively began:

There are nine squares and each one has four edges.
That's 36 edges in all.
If we use three colours, we need three into 36 edges.
That's twelve edges per colour.
And that's the number of individual edges around that array.

No-one cross-examined the logic, some quizzical looks were exchanged and all the group got back on task. This time armed with a belief that the problem could be done, energy was recycled and the problem restarted. Soon frustration percolated the classroom as before, supplying the green edging was proving elusive yet again. There just did not seem to be enough sides on which to pen the green perimeter. It was a different teacher who believed that:

Not every square has to have all three colours on it; surely one or two squares could just have the two colours, red and yellow on them.

No-one seemed to listen, frustration was mounting as successive attempts were made and distracting pleas for economy of paper were often repeated. The group as a whole worked on.

It was the first teacher (again) who later broke the mounting tension, her notion of counting the sides had proved useful. Her partner had suggested trying four squares in a two by two array using just two colours. This she demonstrated (see Figure 9.1a).

Both teachers had unwittingly fallen back on a very important principle, namely that of simplifying a problem. A skill that is often

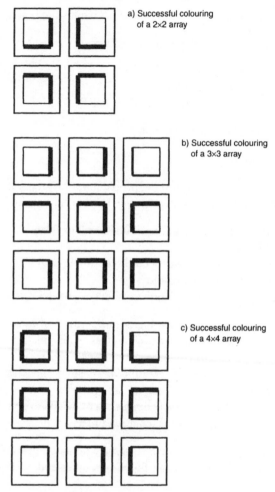

a) Successful colouring
of a 2×2 array

b) Successful colouring
of a 3×3 array

c) Successful colouring
of a 4×4 array

Figure 9.1   Investigating coloured borders
(a) successful colouring of a 2 × 2 array
(b) successful colouring of a 3 × 3 array
(c) successful colouring of a 4 × 4 array

elusive to children, but essential to highlight and encourage when developing children's thinking. Fortified by this insight two teachers reported that they had tried sixteen squares in a four by four array using four colours with consummate ease:

The even numbers are easier than the odds. This array of an even number of squares is easier to colour than an array of odd squares.

This success had restored their belief that a solution to the three by three was possible. It also renewed the overall energies of the remainder of the group, who went back to the task with growing conviction. Some retrod the pathway described by the successful pair of teachers, while others busied themselves with their own developments. Not surprisingly the independent shouts of sheer glee from two different tables heralded the solution to the original problem (see Figure 9.1b).

A different pair of teachers had been just a little more systematic, 'found a pattern' and had produced a different solution (see Figure 9.1c). Comparison between the solutions were made and salient points from within the process of solving the problem were solicited. Not listening, the remainder of the group quickly copied the solution as it was being described. Taking this natural lull in the energy levels to announce lunch, the group were also asked to analyse what they had done that morning and, should they wish it, they were invited to try out the activity with some or all of their respective classes.

It was while clearing away the debris of paper that questions about the morning suggested themselves:

- Could the problem have been presented in a more stimulating way?
- Had enough time and space been allowed for greater ownership of the problem?
- Could I have intervened more and in such a way that more of the group could have shared in the solution of the problem?
- Had I sufficiently encouraged those more successful staff to show, discuss and present work that had been satisfactorily done?

These reflections I would share later with the group, my role as a teacher within that problem-solving environment needed further examination. If we are to enhance children's thinking the role of the teacher needs to be clearly understood. During the morning some of the adults had felt vulnerable, if the situation was to be repeated back at school how could similar feelings in children be minimized if they were to accept the invitation to solve this attractive problem?

Problem solving either as a 'bolt on' to the existing curriculum or as a fully integrated way of working across the entire curriculum, carries with it implications for good primary practice.

- For the staff involved, personal levels of confidence may need to be considered. Any change to a teachers' *modus operandi* when teaching mathematics could cause them personal uncertainty, pose additional insecurity and possibly increase feelings of professional inadequacy. If this were to be the case, then active consideration would need to be given so that staff can:

  - come to terms with what constitutes problem solving in its widest sense;
  - be helped to recognize the virtue a problem solving environment offers to mathematics;
  - be encouraged to be more at ease when problem solving.

  Knowing and understanding the purpose of problem solving could in part counter balance any deficit of confidence whilst a full examination of the teacher's role within a problem solving environment may reassure those concerned.

- Problem solving will challenge existing teaching styles and ensuing approaches to classroom management. Giving consideration to differing ways of working may need to be actively pursued. Is it better to work in smaller groups on specific activities, or perhaps engaging in whole class activities is more appropriate? Maybe there should be opportunities for a mixture of both practices? With the increase in mixed ability grouping, is it better to differentiate by tasks that are set or to seek differentiated outcomes by giving the whole class the same activities to do? More specifically– how do you start a class of children problem solving? Perhaps more importantly is there a need to bring the ensuing activity all together at the end of the lesson(s).

- Are there many activities that are readily available, that can be related to children of all ages and all levels of ability? Or have special provisions to be made so that children of lesser and greater ability can equally benefit? Can problems be simplified or modified in order that children with Special Educational Needs can solve problems without rendering the activity anodyne?

- Assessing more of the learning that takes place within the mathematics classroom is becoming commonplace. Just what do you look for when the children are busy problem solving? What parts of their activity do you focus on and place value upon? How can you know that learning is successfully taking place?

- Can successful problem solving tactics and procedures be specifically taught? Can children be taught to be proficient problem solvers? What strategies can be developed that will foster good problem-solving habits? Are there certain skills that are desirable and useful when problem solving? Is it feasible that a series of specifically chosen problems could be deployed that would help develop a desirable set of problem-solving strategies?

- From the children's point of view, just how welcome is this focusing on problem solving? What fresh insight can be perceived about their mathematical thought processes? Are they more able to apply the skills they have and the items of knowledge they hold? For a subject that appears not to be a universal favourite, what affect on the levels of personal confidence and self-esteem do such problem-solving activities cause? Are the apparent increases in involvement, enjoyment and enthusiasm for the subject sufficient yardsticks against which to measure mathematical competence?

- The subject of mathematics is also under scrutiny with an emphasis now firmly placed on process as opposed to the product. Travelling is often seen as more important than arriving and that mathematical veracity is more to do with an ability to do mathematics at whatever level, than to acquire an ever-widening base of knowledge about the subject.

> An actual formula for the number of squares the diagonal of a rectangle passes through is not, after all, an important thing to possess. The actual process of getting a formula is. (Burton, 1984, p. 60)

Part of a morning with a group of 10- and 11-year-olds

The overlong assembly had caused havoc with lesson plans for the morning. With only 20 minutes of the lesson left, the original plans to investigate 'Happy Numbers' was set aside.

On the flipchart was written: $1 \Omega 3 = 1$ and $2 \Omega 3 = 1$ and the inevitable question was asked: 'what do you think these sums are all about?' From the ready responses – taking a difference was the most common opinion.

So what about: $3 \Omega 3 = ?$

This prompted a very quick reply of 1! There was dismay at seeing the answer:

$3 \Omega 3 = 3$

Discussion seldom strayed far from the idea of difference and that perhaps the rule of keeping the same operation for Ω was not being kept to!

Another sum: $4 \Omega 3 = ?$

Cries of 1 all round. Imagine the delight when on the board was written: $4 \Omega 3 = 1$.

So: $5 \Omega 3 = ?$

The response '2' was there before the question mark. Imagine the chagrin when the sum was completed:

$5 \Omega 3 = 1$

'What then is $6 \Omega 3$ equal to if a difference is not being taken?'

To help along the thinking processes the results so far were collated separately on the blackboard:

$1 \Omega 3 = 1$

$2 \Omega 3 = 1$

$3 \Omega 3 = 3$

$4 \Omega 3 = 1$

$5 \Omega 3 = 1$

$6 \Omega 3 = ?$ 'Is there a pattern?'

Three was the rejoinder to this hollow question. The pattern was going one, one, three!

Quickly more questions were added to the flipchart:

$9 \Omega 3 =$

$10 \Omega 3 =$

$13 \Omega 3 =$

$16 \Omega 3 =$

In turn the answers were given but after a lot of mumblings and mutterings about

'... it goes into ... and there is that left over ...'

'3'

'1'

'1'

'1'

'Could some say how they were working out the answers?'

Near to the back of the group, two children were busy with paper and pencil and poring over a times table chart.

Darren spoke: 'You divide the first number by the last number, if there is a remainder you write that as the answer, if there isn't a remainder then the answer is 3.'

'OK. let's test your idea':

$14 \, \Omega \, 3 = ?$

Cries of '2' were randomly repeated around the room.

'NO!'

$14 \, \Omega \, 3 = 1$

It was Vicky who spoke, as she had been working with Darren: 'You divide the first number by the 3, if it goes in exactly then the answer is 3, if there is a remainder then the answer is always 1.'

To put the latest opinion to the test the group were invited to make up some questions to which the answers would be given. They asked:

$15 \, \Omega \, 3 = ?; 17 \, \Omega \, 3 = ?; 18 \, \Omega \, 3 = ?; 20 \, \Omega \, 3 = ?; 22 \, \Omega \, 3 = ?;$ and $25 \, \Omega \, 3 = ?$

The answers given did in fact fit the conjecture Vicky had made:

'1, 1, 3, 1, 1 and 1'

The confidence of the group visibly swelled. But, on a fresh sheet of the flipchart was written:

$1 \, \Omega \, 4 = 1$

$2 \, \Omega \, 4 = 2$

$3 \, \Omega \, 4 = ?$

It was explained that Ω still meant the same as before, and it was pointed out that Vicky and Darren's idea was alright in as far as it went but it needed to be adapted to work with last numbers other than three.

'So what about $3 \, \Omega \, 4 = ?$' It was unanimously agreed '3.' The explanation was '... that 4 divided into 3 is nought remainder 3.'

Onto the flipchart the answer was added:

$3 \, \Omega \, 4 = 1$

All were surprised and a small cry 'it is the difference', was heard again.

The next question was added:

$4 \, \Omega \, 4 = ?$

To which everyone agreed was equal to '4', and relief at getting right was felt.

Quickly a list of questions were posted for the children to work at, to discuss amongst themselves and then share with the whole group:

5 Ω 4 =

6 Ω 4 =

7 Ω 4 =

8 Ω 4 =

12 Ω 4 =

14 Ω 4 =

17 Ω 4 =

Answers were forthcoming, because at the tables there had obviously been much visible activity – lots of scribbling and crossings out, many ideas had been sounded out and opinions argued:

'1, 2, 1, 4, 4, 2, and 1'

Getting the right answers was a sure-fire way of building up personal confidences, the children had clearly spotted another pattern and built on it as they had done with the Ω 3. A firm foundation had been laid for additional work, but would the group or some of the individuals within it be able to generalize from it the concept of Highest Common Factor?

At the end of the lesson I reflected on both the teachers' reactions and those of the children. To the question of, 'What is problem solving?', a common thread which ran through the teachers' perceptions was the ability to bring previous knowledge to bear on unfamiliar situations. Could I have helped the children more to reconstruct what they already knew, which would have given them improved access to HCFs?

Another problem – some student teachers doing LOGO – more steps in turtle geometry

Perhaps a more readily available access to problem solving is that associated with the computer language LOGO. Only a little teacher input is required to give the student access to problem solving, where newly-found knowledge can be put to good use.

An earlier school experience had very briefly introduced some of this group of student teachers to the Floor Turtle. These teacher trainees, within differing cross-curricular contexts, had been involved in drawing out on large sheets of paper different scenes from other lessons: e.g. an outline of an aeroplane; two rabbits in a garden; boats on the river; an articulated lorry; a railway engine and small station, etc.

A few others in the group had worked in a similar small way with other programmable toys – *Roamer*, *Pip* and *Big Track*. These they had manœuvred around specific obstacle courses: e.g. a cross-country event for horses, negotiating around a housing estate, playing 'follow my leader', hopping around the lily pads of a pond.

A reminder about the primitives Forward and Right (Turn) was given to the group before a volunteer was asked to walk a square. The walk was to be completed in pigeon steps (i.e. with one foot in front of the other) in the large space available within the computer suite.

> go for'rard 20 steps ...
> now do a quarter turn ...
> forwards 20 steps ...
> now another quarter turn ...
> twenty steps ...
> finally a quarter turn ...
> and 20 steps ...

The convention of returning a person (screen turtle/programmable toy) to their original position pre-empted the final response: 'and a quarter turn'. With the equivalence of 90 degrees and a quarter turn rapidly established the previous verbal responses were recorded schematically on the board:

> FD 20 RT 90
> FD 20 RT 90
> FD 20 RT 90
> FD 20 RT 90

Which after a brief discussion, was then revised accordingly:

> REPEAT 4 [FD 20 RT 90]

The group was then invited to complete the following task: on your screen draw either three squares, each of a different size and of a different orientation or any other design of their choosing.

The original intention had been to:

- remind them of the need for additional primitives to go BACK-WARDS (by specific amounts), turn LEFT (in varying degrees), use PENUP (to allow subsequent movement without leaving a trace on the screen) and PENDOWN, CLEARSCREEN, HIDETURTLE and HOME (returns screen turtle to the centre of screen) conventionally abbreviated to BK, LT, PU, PD, CS , HT, HOME

- encourage the building of procedures which could be used time and again;

- develop an appreciation of certain conventions needed to drive the Logo program efficiently.

The above had been successfully realized, with an unexpected development of an emerging need for a working knowledge of variables. Within a half-hour the additional primitives to EDALL and ERALL had also proved useful and most students were eventually at ease with procedures like the following and their attendant conventions:

```
TO SQUARE 'SIDE
REPEAT 4 [FD :SIDE RT 90]
END
```

This allowed them to draw any number of squares of any size, anywhere on the screen: e.g.

```
SQUARE 60 LT 120 SQUARE −80
SQUARE 45 RT 65 PU FD 70 PD SQUARE 85 HOME
SQUARE 20 RT 30 SQUARE 50 RT 40 SQUARE 80 RT 50
SQUARE 100 RT 70 SQUARE 120
```

A series of visual starters were then given to the students to choose from that would allow them concrete access to what they had previously learnt and hopefully made sense of, and allow them to solve related problems.

They were to attempt the problem of writing procedures or a program (a suite of procedures) that would generate one of the designs. The final part of the session would be an examination of what they had done and how they had gone about it.

From the viewpoint of the observer there appeared to be three stages to the activity that ensued:

Figure 9.2 Patterns for investigating using LOGO.

- An *Initiation* stage wherein many of the student teachers began the planning of the chosen task, breaking it down into smaller controllable items, checking out individual ideas to be used and depending on feedback – reviewing the work undertaken. Most students generally worked with paper and pencil as opposed to those who originally worked on the chosen design direct at the computer keyboard and who were rapidly frustrated by the computer's inability to perform the task.

- A *Doing* stage wherein the student teachers, having selected the ideas they wanted to bring together, worked methodically at their chosen procedures. They were constantly reviewing, refining and representing them as the trialling of their ideas did or did not work. This was in contrast with those students who had worked directly at the computer who were finding the process of reacting to mistakes a messy affair as work being trialled was being lost or overwritten.

- A *Concluding* period wherein some of the group checked work done, enabling them to sit back and find ways of 'tidying' up what they had devised.

But how had they reacted to the task?

- They had found that drawing/sketching their chosen designs had given them an overall foothold to the task. It had enabled them to become familiar with what was needed and where parts of their designs could start and finish.

- They had been surprised how, with such a little amount of new-found knowledge, they were able to build so much on it. This they also contrasted with their existing knowledge of mathematics, whose lack of applicability if anything detracted from their general level of confidence.

- The designs – the problems to be solved, were accessible and not obtuse or hidden amongst a welter of words to be carefully analysed for clues.

- That perceptibly there was no right or wrong ways of doing the designs – just conventions to be mastered when writing procedures. In consequence the tension of 'solving the problems' had been removed and in its place had grown a personal challenge to control the computer and get it to do what was required.

- They had not considered the activity as anything mathematical!

In summation, the most impressive dimension of the morning had been the development of personal autonomy through this excursion into Turtle Geometry. They felt in control of what they had done and could appreciate the benefits to personal confidence that this 'exercising of skills' had caused! There was also an acknowledgement that some mathematical perspective had filtered through.

Perhaps the role of the teacher in the problem-solving environment is to help pupils reconstruct their own valid pathways to solutions. The teachers at the beginning felt vulnerable and threatened, the children had not, perhaps trusting the teacher to know better. In contrast the student teachers had felt more in control while working with the computer. How can the teacher fulfil the role of delivering the learner from the threat of vulnerability to the feeling of being in control within a problem-solving situation? The attractiveness of the problem, to whet the curiosity and provide motivation might be one more very important dimension.

Using and applying mathematics

Group 8 at a recent Primary Mathematics Teacher's Conference in the UK had just one session in the afternoon, in which to explore some of the issues connected with 'Using and Applying Mathematics' – one of the Attainment Targets in the Mathematics National Curriculum for England and Wales (DES/WO, 1989). The task chosen to focus the attention of the group had been an 'elimination' shuffle. A pack of ten playing cards numbered one (ace) to ten are arranged in a particular order. They are shuffled according to a specific routine. The cards are then taken singularly from the top of the pack and placed underneath. As the routine is carried out the numbers one to ten are to be spelt out. These two operations completed simultaneously:

'O' card taken from pack and put underneath;
'N' card taken from pack and put underneath;
'E' card taken from pack, shown – it is the ace (1) and is placed face up on the table;
'T' card taken from pack and put underneath;
'W' card taken from pack and put underneath;
'O' card taken from pack, shown – it is the two (2) and is placed face up on the table.

163

This routine was followed until all ten cards had been laid out in numerical order on the table. Packs of cards were available for staff to begin the task. How to begin? No-one there admitted to having knowledge or experience of the 'mathematics of playing cards', but all conceded an ability to spell.

Most at first tried to sort out their chosen cards in the hand, with the face value of the cards fanning out in ascending order:

But the one comes out third ...
And the two comes fifth, no sixth ...
Yes, where does the last 'E' in three go?

There was much confusion as differing arrangements of ten cards were being shuffled and spelt out. 'Trial and improvement is a valid technique', was the much used statement! Initially, all had a modest amount of success, with the respective arrangements faltering after the third or fourth card had been declared 'E' or 'R'! While some other pairs of teachers tried the activity for smaller packs of cards.

After these *failures* (their word) the notion of a circular arrangement of the cards appeared to spread through the group and that the secret appeared to be to count on. From whence it came no-one was prepared to admit, but it allowed people to put a more favourable structure to the original task. Some arranged their work around a ten-pointed clock face while others had a line, along which they counted repeatedly.

It was not long after that several pairs of teachers had an arrangement for the cards that worked and this was readily compared and shared with the whole group: i.e. 3, 5, 1, 8, 10, 2, 4, 6, 7, 9. Satisfied that the problem had been laid bare, the group were than asked: 'Having done so well, how would you build on this activity?'

Brief discussion followed and suggestions were quickly made and recorded:

continue the sequence adding 11, 12 and 13 for a suit of cards;
add in the jack, queen, king; (how would these differ?)
repeat for the whole pack of cards one ... king, one ... king, etc.;
translating the activity into French words un, deux ...;
into German;
Urdu and Gujerati;
Welsh

pulling out the cards alternately re'D', blac'K', re'D' ...;
or diamond'S', club'S', heart'S', Spade'S' ....

There was adequate time for the teachers to select an activity from
the above and work at their chosen task(s). The intention was that later
on, consideration would be given to: *What had they been doing with special
reference to Using and Applying Mathematics?*

Eventually putting aside their recent successes with 'elimination'
shuffles and aware of the stages of development associated with Level
Descriptions in the English and Welsh National Curriculum the staff,
after protracted discussion and moderation of their efforts, decided
they had achieved:

> Level 5 ... identify and obtain necessary information; ... check results,
> considering whether they are sensible ... show understanding of situations
> by describing them mathematically using symbols, words and diagrams ...
> make conjectures ... based on evidence ... produced, and give a convin-
> cing explanation of their reasoning.

> Level 6 ... carry through substantial tasks and solve quite complex
> problems by breaking them down into more manageable tasks. ... inter-
> pret, discuss and synthesize information ... appreciate the need to question
> the accuracy of generalizations and test them by checking a few particular
> cases. (SCAA, 1994, p. 24)

Perhaps more importantly they had enjoyed the problem and the
apparently natural extensions to it. All of which appeared to allow
them the autonomy to devise, design and plan their own mathematical
ways through the tasks undertaken.

All of the original questions posed near the beginning of this
chapter are those which have beset teachers over the last decade.
Many colleagues are still looking for suitable answers. Establishing the
problem-solving classroom has not been widely accepted in schools, in
spite of a real desire from educators that it be so. It can be seen that it is
not an easy task. The teachers, pupils and trainee teachers who have
taken part in the activities above have learned something about their
tasks, but more importantly something about their own abilities to
cope in these situations. The importance of this dimension must be
realized before we can ask children to do the same. Perhaps what is
needed is a drive to allow teachers themselves to become confident
problem solvers, not only on their own, but in interaction with others.

All of the problems here are of different types, which give rise to different skills and perspectives. This may mitigate against the idea that problem solving can be taught. Genuine problem solving is dependent on activity which enhances existing skills further, giving a basis to build fresh skills and insights. Perhaps one underlying prerequisite which can be cited is tenacity, the ability to stick with what is uncertain, to try out different strategies. The ability to spot pattern, be systematic, be able to predict and prove then generalize are intrinsic to the skills of the problem solver. Yet can these attributes be taught? Or are they acquired through practice? Above all there must exist the emotional desire to solve problems, the ability to 'stay with it'. The teacher will never understand the implications of this for children unless s/he has tried it for themselves.

If we are to enhance children's thinking within the context of a problem-solving environment there would appear certain good housekeeping routines that can be fostered. These can be broadly grouped into three distinct phases:

1. An *initial phase* concerned with entering the problem wherein relevant information about the problem is distilled, certain aspects selected, reorganized, represented and, if necessary, redefined and recorded. It is the time to consider what techniques are applicable and what methods would apply to the problem. It is the time when parallels and past experiences with previous problems can be usefully recycled. In short, it is about getting started, becoming involved and mulling over the problem, deciding what the essential features are and what ways forward there could be. The need is for a plan of attack!

2. The *middle phase* is for attacking the problem. This is the time to try out initial reactions and ideas developed as a consequence. To go on to abandon those ideas that do not work and simplify those that give only limited success, while constantly refining those that do work successfully. It is a time for systematic working and the diligent searching for what is happening. The need is to break the problem down into relevant parts and analyse each part separately, to check ideas used, and begin manipulating those skills that the problem solver already possesses. It is the time when insights about the problem will be developed, it is when early modest success can often lead onto a wider understanding of the problem. It is when assumptions made and refined are based on observable evidence. It is the time to formulate

and test conjectures about the problem. What is really happening? Is there any relation between the inputs and outputs to the problem? Can what is observed be justified? Does the relation always hold true?

3. A *final phase* of reviewing work undertaken. The need is to look back and check the logic and structure of the work undertaken. Are you convinced by what has been found and observed? Are there patterns to the results obtained? Have errors been made and can they be rectified? Did the original plan of attack work? Perhaps more importantly, can what is observed be extended to other similar problems? It is the time to convince oneself that a solution to the problem has been found and to think of ways in which others could be persuaded of the rightness to the solution.

REFERENCES

Burton, L. (1984) *Thinking Things Through*. Oxford: Basil Blackwell.
DES (1989) *Mathematics in the National Curriculum*. London: HMSO.
SCAA (1994) *Mathematics in the National Curriculum: Draft Proposals*. London: SCAA.
DES (1989) *Mathematics in the National Curriculum – Non-Statutory Guidance*. London: HMSO.

Name Index

Name Index

Subject Index

abstract   28–9, 79, 111, 114, 115, 134
  nature of tasks   21
  symbolism   17
  representations   28, 31
abstraction   46, 120, 140, 145
accommodation   4
addition   128–31, 135–7
  processes of   32
  solving problems in   93, 96
  strategy for   24
  sums   37
  symbol for   77
  using function machines   140–3
algebra   37, 124–147
algorithms   93, 127, 143
  for long multiplication   130
  standard written   27, 35
  for subtraction   64
algorithmic approach   90
alphanumeric   120
ambiguity   55, 72
  linguistic   56
anxiety   96, 102
approximators   70–72
arithmetic   1, 127, 129–30
  calculations   13
  calculator   89
  concepts   101
  logic   140, 145
  process   135
  skills   145
  symbols of   90
  teaching of   74–8, 127
array   152
assessment   87, 103, 154
Assessment of Performance Unit
  (APU)   13, 103
assimilation   4
associative   128–31
attitude   9, 63
  to art   92
  changed   94
  of students   101
attributes   112, 117, 120
auonomy   165

balance method   136, 142–5
behaviourist   3
bilingual   61
Big Track   159
binary tree   118
bolt on   153
Brazilian street children   13, 26

calculation   77, 89, 96, 137–9
  children's methods   75
  children's own methods   27, 35
  complex   74
  computer   131, 147
  horizontal   21
  mental   13, 24, 35, 93, 96–9, 107,
    128–9
  of multiplication   81
  procedures   91
  written symbolic   83
calculator   7, 88–90, 92–109
  in society   1–2, 75
  logic   140
  use of   32, 129, 145
Carroll diagrams   113–6
cartesian product   43, 52
chunking   21
closed   130
collaborate   8, 38, 94
collaborative work   150
combinatorial   49, 52
communication   41–2, 54–5, 61, 72
commutative   37, 128–31
competence   57
complement   129
computational methods   67
computer   7, 75
  in the classroom   38
  databases   117–23
  LOGO   158–63
  packages   114, 131
  program   65, 117
  software   110
concepts   6
confidence   2, 6, 12, 28, 94
  group   157

171

Subject Index